WOVEN STYLE FOR THE 15" RIGID HEDDLE LOOM

Add Sewing, Knitting, & Crochet to Go Beyond the Rectangle

Tamara Poff

 Poff Studio

Copyright © 2016 Tamara Poff
ISBN: 978-0-9984590-0-4

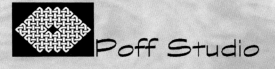 Poff Studio

Summerfield, Florida 34491

www.poffstudio.com

Layout and Design: Tamara Poff

Art Direction: Jill Greenop

Editor: Heidi Sunday

Technical Editor: Lynn Lee

Photographers: Jill Greenop and Christopher Roth

Dedication page photo: Laura Musikanski

Skills Icons: Sergey Demushkin, the Noun Project

Knitting symbols and fit chart source:

Craft Yarn Council of America, www.YarnStandards.com

© 2016 Tamara Poff

ACKNOWLEDGMENTS

Many thanks to the following yarn companies for their generous donations: Blue Heron Yarns, Colinton Australia, Hamilton Yarns, Interlacements Yarns, Mango Moon Yarns, and Plymouth Yarn Company.

Also grateful acknowledgment to Jane Patrick and Judy Pagels of Schacht Spindle Company for their advice and support.

Lastly, loving thanks to my dearly departed, Tom and Peg Burt for their DNA, and to Mark Poff, Ashley Milhizer, Chris Perry, and Alix Booms for all their time, beauty, and devotion.

Contents

Patterns

Resources

This book is dedicated to local yarn shops everywhere who struggle passionately to share the joy of handcrafting in this ever changing culture, and to my students who fuel my own creative energies!

Introduction

As a floor loom weaver, a knitter, and an all-over fiber enthusiast from decades back, I never dreamed that I would fall so completely for the portable, rigid heddle loom. As a teacher of this simple weaving tool throughout Florida, Georgia, and Michigan in the last several years, I've helped place 100's of the small looms in the hands of new weavers throughout the eastern time zone. Although we love scarves, I feel a deep sense of responsibility to these folks to take them beyond viewing the small loom as only a scarf making machine.

I see the 15" rigid heddle as a perfect portal for endless creation in our "on the go" society. I have taken my little loom to work in hotels, to family gatherings, and to social events throughout the country. I've even done a little weaving in the car...as a passenger, and ok, I had a deadline! We can produce beautiful wearables so quickly. One of my mantras is, "weave it today, wash it tonight, wear it tomorrow", albeit somewhat damp.

For all of the reasons above, I consider the rigid heddle as the craft tool of our times. In this book, I strive for simple and stylish designs that I can feel comfortable wearing everyday and that I think my students will find just as wearable. Although I've covered some expanded techniques such as pick-up patterns, alternative warps, and multiple shuttle handling, the emphasis is on simple construction using mostly plain weave to showcase the beautiful yarns found inside local yarn shops.

The garments herein will incorporate basic sewing, knitting, and very elementary crochet skills in varied amounts. The knitting skills required are all at an easy rating except for the Boat Neck Top with Sleeves (p.50) and the Ashley Vest (p.72) which I will rate Intermediate knitting due to shaping and yarn overs for the former, and larger stitch count and short rows for the later. Crochet provides a super finish to sharpen edges. If you don't know the basics, take a class, or check out the internet, and you'll have what you need for these designs.

This is a pattern and skill book for beginning weavers and beyond, who can warp and weave on their own and want to take their product to the next level. To learn more about weaving fundamentals, there are all kinds of great online videos, classes, and books, along with support from your favorite yarn shop to get you started quite handily. For a selection of my favorite books and videos on the subject, please see the bibliography p.94.

If you've attended my classes, you know that I teach some rather quirky approaches to traditional techniques. My journey of discovery, with my student's enthusiastic input, has led to some "off road handling" of finishing and weaving methodology. I hope this will inspire your own exploration. The greatest allure of this craft is that there is so much room for invention!

So get ready for a pattern book of the teaching kind: conversational in style with lots of musings, tips, and tricks to give you an added perspective of the why, the how, and the alternatives as you grow your weaving skills.

Start Here

(No, really! This is Important)

I know you're anxious to dive in, but I promised you "quirky" techniques, and much of that will be found from here to p.30. Let's spend some time getting familiar with the topics of this section. Then you can get on with it, agreed? I've done a little underlining of key phrases and concepts throughout to help you with focus.

One of my goals here is to show that simple tools can create beautiful results. If your budget allows more sophisticated tools, you are fortunate. If not, this won't slow you down.

You'll find instruction, both old and new, as it applies to the patterns. Need more advice? I've given you a personally reviewed bibliography on page 94 to expand your practice.

Equipment

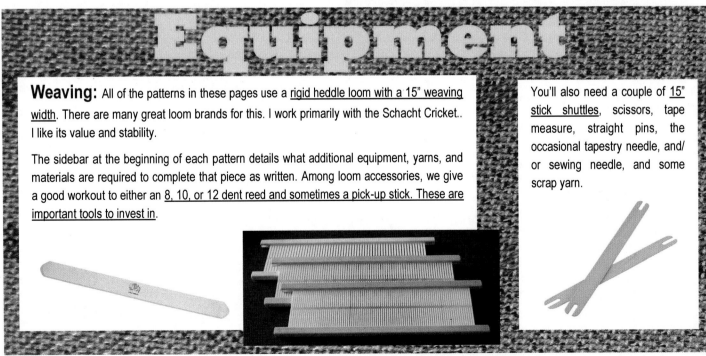

Weaving: All of the patterns in these pages use a rigid heddle loom with a 15" weaving width. There are many great loom brands for this. I work primarily with the Schacht Cricket.. I like its value and stability.

The sidebar at the beginning of each pattern details what additional equipment, yarns, and materials are required to complete that piece as written. Among loom accessories, we give a good workout to either an 8, 10, or 12 dent reed and sometimes a pick-up stick. These are important tools to invest in.

You'll also need a couple of 15" stick shuttles, scissors, tape measure, straight pins, the occasional tapestry needle, and/ or sewing needle, and some scrap yarn.

Warp Sticks

Each time you warp your loom, you will need packing between the layers of yarn. This keeps the yarn from forming hills and valleys for the yarn to fall into that would create problems with tension.

I buy rolls of kraft paper at a dollar store to cut to size for this. Whenever I warp wider than 13", I like to use warp sticks instead (or alternate warp sticks with pieces of paper packing). This minimizes the chance that the warp threads at either end will fall off the sides of the paper and mess up your selvedges. You'll also fight less with the paper bunching up at edges as you roll.

Although they can be purchased, I like to cut my own sticks. I take artist's mat board or balsa wood from the craft store, a metal ruler, and a utility knife, and cut sticks about 7/8" deep x the width of the loom's back beam. A good fit is key. Use up the space on the back beam, but not so tight they get stuck. Plain old cardboard is useful and abundant for these, but does get shop worn more quickly.

I stagger the sticks, placing one about every couple inches between the yarn layers on the warp beam as I wind on.

Although a floor stand is not required, it is very useful to be able to weave anywhere and to adjust your working angle.

Sewing

I use a very basic sewing machine these days. My designs require no more than straight and zig zag lines. I don't have the heart to attack carefully woven fabric with the invasiveness of a buttonhole from my simple machine, so where you see buttons, they are just the cover up for hand applied snaps. If you have an automatic buttonhole option on your machine, you many want to weave some scrap fabric with your piece and try it first.

My main concern is that the machine be good at handling both lightweight and weighty handmade fabrics without chewing them up I am pleased with the Babylock BL9, an entry level model. I use this with a walking foot to accommodate heavier fabric and multiple thicknesses.

Whatever machine you use, try it with some handmade scrap before you get serious or see your local retailer for advice. Stitch length varies by yarn weight (finer fiber, shorter stitch) and preference. Handwovens don't like to be overworked if you need to rip out, so be mindful of backstitching or very short stitches unless you are confident the seam is final.

You'll also need a good iron and ironing board. With a glance at your yarn label for care, weaving needs and tolerates more steam pressing than knitting or crochet.

WEAVING TERMS & ABBREVIATIONS

Apron rod: rod that holds warp ties and loops on the loom.

Apron string: attaches the apron rod to the loom.

Beat: to push weft threads into place. This is often a misnomer since most yarns will only need a nudge into place to achieve the ppi given in the patterns and for optimal drape.

Cloth Beam: the front beam that the fabric rolls onto as you weave.

Dent: openings (per inch) in the reed.

Draw-In: The difference between the warp width in the reed and the fabric width as you weave the fabric. Your fabric will frequently draw-in by 10% of the warp width.

End: one strand of warp.

Epi: ends per inch (number of warp threads in an inch of warp width).

Fell Line: the last pick you beat into place. We pay attention to fell line and make adjustments to our beat to make this as perfectly horizontal as possible.

Felting: to subject fabric to hot water and extreme agitation to create a fabric that holds together as a solid mass.

Fulling: or to "full" is to cause the fibers to plump while washing to make them stronger and warmer. Involves some agitation and higher water temps. Extreme fulling is felting.

Heddle or Rigid Heddle: going back to my floor loom days, this is the vertical piece on the reed with a hole that holds a warp thread. Used interchangeably with reed in our world.

Pick: one pass of weft through a shed; one row in knitter's terms.

Ppi: picks per inch (number of weft rows or shots per inch of weaving).   .

Reed: the device made up of heddles with holes and slots. The reed moves the hole yarn up or down to open a shed, controls the warp sett, and is used to beat the weft.

Selvedge: a vertical side edge of weaving.

Sett: spacing of threads/inch. Warp sett is determined by your reed and is expressed as your epi. Weft sett is determined by your beat and is expressed as your ppi.

Shed: opening between the warp threads created by raising (up shed) or lowering (down shed) the reed or heddle.

Shuttle: holds the weft to pass through the shed. I prefer a stick shuttle for the 15" loom.

Sley: to pull warp threads through the hole in the heddle.

Take-up: the extra yarn used as warp and weft threads bend over and under each other.

Throw: to pass the Shuttle through the open shed.

Warp Beam: the beam that the warp rolls around on the back of the loom.

Warp (woof): the vertical threads placed first onto the loom. Also the process of putting the vertical threads on the loom.

Weft: the horizontal threads passed through an open shed.

KNITTING ABBREVIATIONS

Dec: decrease

In: inches

Inc: increase

K: knit

K2 tog: knit 2 stitches together

M1: make 1 stitch. In this book, we will use a backwards loop cast on to make 1.

P: purl

P2tog: purl 2 stitches together

Pm: place marker

Rs: right side

Sl: slip

Ssk: slip 2 stitches individually as if to knit. Insert left hand needle into the front of these stitches and knit them together.

St(s): stitch(es)

Ws: wrong side

Yd(s): yard(s)

Yo: yarn over

CROCHET ABBREVIATIONS

Ch: chain

Hdc: half double crochet

Rnd(s): round(s)

Sc: single crochet

Skills added

At the bottom of each sidebar, I have indicated the needlecrafting skills that are incorporated in that design with the icons at right.

Knitting

Crochet

Machine Sewing

Hand Stitching

11

More About Materials

Yarns used in these designs are detailed on pages 96-97. Should you wish to substitute, yardage is given in the charts at the beginning of each pattern.

If you have any doubt about your choices, I strongly recommend sampling. You may save yourself a lot of yarn, time, and frustration by weaving a quick swatch. My YouTube video, "Test Warp on the Rigid Heddle Loom" will demonstrate a quick and frugal way to do your swatch using as little as 22" for warp length. As recommended there, a 6" test warp width is a minimum to test color and fabric. If you have enough extra for an 8" width, all the better to insure accurate gauge.

You can also test for the results of your yarn choices at the beginning of your weaving. You may want to add to the warp length for this. You may also want to add enough to create an extra sample piece for dabbling with on your sewing machine. Of course, with live testing like this, you have already committed to a few hundred yards of warp. At least you can change your mind on weft if you are not happy. Don't be afraid to change horses if your weft plan is not working.

One way recommended to determine a balanced warp and weft sett for a yarn is to wrap it around a ruler and divide the number of wraps per inch by 2. Because that can be influenced by how tight you feel like wrapping yarn that day, and yarns perform differently, I give you my thought process for gauge guidelines on the next page. Pay attention to the way the yarn responds for balance and stability, and adjust as necessary.

Video Support

For a variety of helpful, short videos, check out and subscribe to my channel, "Poff Studio", at *YouTube.com*. These are also posted on my website, www.poffstudio.com. If you are so inclined, please like, share, and let me know your thoughts!

EPI and PPI

The epi, or ends per inch, given in the patterns is simply your reed sett. Note the ppi in each pattern. This is the number of picks in each inch under tension to achieve desired results. After weaving at least an inch of your piece, measure along a visible warp thread to see if the under + over weft threads make gauge. Also, once you've established the draw-in appropriate to your fabric (optimal selvedges, p.19), measure the weaving width to record this measurement.

It may take 2-3" after you start weaving before your draw-in is consistent because the knots will hold your edges out. Once established, use this information to check your work any time you worry about keeping consistency while you weave.

Also, advance your fabric often - about every 2-3". Your reed will hold your edges outward and distort selvedges if you weave too close to it.

Notes About Gauge and Fiber Combination

On most little looms, you have 4 different reed sizes available: 5, 8 (or 7.5), 10, and 12 dent reeds. These numbers simply indicate how many single vertical (warp) threads you can achieve with that reed. This is the sett for your epi. We'll use 3 reed sizes in this book. If you are using substitute yarns, here's how I look at the 3 choices:

The 8 dent works well for worsted weight warps and for many dk weights.

The 12 dent is generally for fingering, sport gauge and some lace weight. This means lace yarn that is stiffer or "stickier" like linens, cottons, and hairier animal fibers (or blends thereof) that won't allow the weft to beat down as easily as slippery bamboos, silk, merino, and rayon. Slippery lace weights may not be well suited to the little loom, but can be doubled to try on the 10 or 12 dent reed. If you double yarn as you direct warp, pull a loop through a slot and the next through a hole, and you won't have to sley the reed separately. If you are disappointed that you chose a warp that was too fine once you start, you can try doubling your weft as you wind onto your shuttle and still get some interesting results.

I call the 10 dent the "middle guy". It is great for stepping down dk (especially slippery dk's) for a more stable fabric. It also works for stepping up a stickier sport gauge for a little more air in there. Brushed, lace weight, mohair generally rocks the 10 dent reed due to its sticky nature.

Wearables require a little air between the fibers to achieve optimal drape. This means you should work towards a balance between the vertical and the horizontal threads. Example: worsted weight yarn on an 8 dent reed achieves the best drape at 8 ppi.

13

Gauge and Fiber Combination Continued

I often use a lace weight weft with a heavier gauge warp for added drape and softness, even though this may throw off the weft to warp balance concept. <u>Strike a happy medium between a "too tight" beat for your garment fabric and one so light that it creates unstable fabric with threads that shift or distort</u>, and you will be fine. The right beat comes with experience using different yarns, so keep weaving, and remember that woven fabric contracts when removed from the loom to get tighter.

When combining yarns, I frequently avoid pairing plant fiber (cotton, linen, hemp) with animal fibers (wool, alpaca, mohair). I notice rayon seems to live well in both worlds. Although there are some notable exceptions (some in this book), I give this careful consideration in my choices. Maybe that's just me, so feel free to experiment to your taste.

Also <u>be wary about putting yarns that have dramatically different gauges in the same warp</u>. This can result in some puckering of the fabric. Likewise varying yarn gauges in the same weft can create wavy edges. Either way, this is due to differing take-up and draw-in, and the problem may not show until your piece is removed from the loom. There are variable reeds with segmented pieces that allow multiple gauge yarns in your warp, but they limit your options for striping to specific increments, so I don't use mine extensively. Keeping the inclusion of the odd weight yarns to a minimum and isolating them to very narrow stripes or bands can help you get away with this.

Lastly, I think it helps to have <u>a color system</u> to work with. I like Laura Bryant's, "A Fiber Artist's Guide to Color". See Videos, p. 95. She identifies the problems associated with color and value, gives yarn colors weight, and defines some guidelines we can use for selection.

Yarns and Yarn Weight

I look at rigid heddle weaving from a knitter's perspective: that everything in your local yarn shop can be weaving material when used correctly. There are a few cautions for warp. Beware of yarns that break easily when held about 10-12" apart as they won't hold up under tension. Also, avoid elastic content that will stretch and then pucker your weaving (unless that is the desired result).

Mohair is a challenge, but can create beautiful work. When using mohair, choose the shorter fiber versions and be prepared to do battle to keep the warp from felting together and closing your shed, p.20.

I've incorporated the yarn weights at right, with knitting gauge and symbols from The Craft Yarn Council. For more detailed information, see *www.craftyarncouncil/weight.html*

Lace
33-40 sts/in on US 000-1

Fingering or Sock
27-32 sts/in on US 1-3

Sport
23-26 sts/in on US 3-5

DK or Light Worsted
21-24 sts/in on US 5-7

FIT: Easy as ABC

I think that it is crucial to locate your favorite fitting top, jacket, poncho, and scarf. Collect the measurements from these that you will use to adjust patterns to your individual shape. Most of the garments in this book have a very general fit with the key measurements being:

A: length from shoulder at neck to bottom edge.

B: the fullest part of bust. The difference between "to fit bust size" and "finished measurement at bust" in the pattern specifications is the ease that characterizes that design. The Craft Yarn Council's Fit Chart is shown below right for the standards used.

C: widest point at hip. If your hip measurement exceeds your bust measurement, take a look at options offering a side vent for further ease so you can still get a good fit at bust.

Keep an up-to-date journal with your measurements, along with test swatches and lots of notes on your results. Document the gauges, fiber blends, yarn brands, weave sett etc. This time spent will save you hours later.

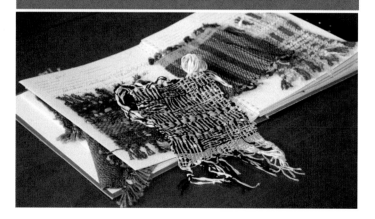

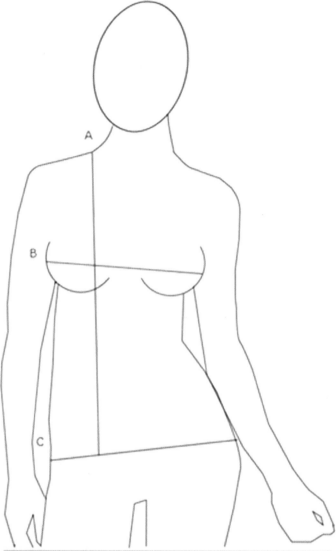

Fit Chart	
Very-close fitting:	Actual chest/bust measurement or less
Close-fitting:	1–2"/2.5–5cm
Standard-fitting:	2–4"/5–10cm
Loose-fitting:	4–6"/10–15cm Oversized: 6"/15cm or more

The Warp and the "Woof"

Chart Reading, Warp Order

When warping requires color or pattern changes, charts like the one shown below tell you the number of ends (not loops) to sley as you warp. This chart is read right to left if you choose to start your warp from the right (typical for right handers) or read left to right (left handers). This represents how you proceed to set up your warp changes as you face the back of the loom.

In this case, the chart tells you to start with the main color and work 16 ends for the small (8 loops in slots during direct warping). The numbers in parenthesis are for the size changes. After you complete that count, the chart indicates a yarn change to the contrast color. Run 2 ends (1 loop) of contrast, then 2 ends (1 loop) of main color. The sequence outlined with bold line will be repeated (4x = 4 times) before continuing to the left.

When alternating one loop of yarn with a loop of another yarn, I find that I do not need to cut and tie the start and end of my color changes onto the apron rod each time. I can carry the color changes along by sliding the last color drawn to the left and out of the way as I work. OTHERWISE, I strongly suggest that you cut and tie every color change when you have to cross more than one loop. This will avoid troublesome crossing in the back that can interfere with the clean opening of your shed later. If you do find that crossing threads in the back tend to close your shed opening, see p.20, troubleshooting.

		4x		4x		4x		
Main Color	16 (18, 20, 24, 26,26)	2	22	2	22	2		16 (18, 20, 24, 26,26)
Contrast			2	2	2	2	2	2

16

Weaving Order

There are many ways to describe the order of weaving. When there are a lot of weaving changes, I like to use a graph as shown at right (taken from the tote bag on p.86). This is read from top to bottom for color or pattern changes as you weave.

Imagine weaving a fancy scarf with a lot of color changes. Then imagine that you want it to hang to match on the other side after it goes around your neck. You could record your path (top-down) on the first end, then simply reverse your weaving, reading from the bottom-up of this chart to create the other end. Voila!

Multi	Solid
2-3/4"	
	2-1/4"
8-3/4"	
	2-1/4"
4-1/2"	
	2-1/4"
8-3/4"	
	2-1/4"
2-3/4"	

More about Warping

I use the direct warping method (pulling loops starting from the back of the loom to the warping peg) throughout. Given the few yards we use, this avoids the need for the extra expense and effort of the warping board used with indirect warping. The greatest distance you will need is around 14' for the linen lace top.

Some weavers like to use a warping board when calculating an odd number of warp ends, rather than pulling loops directly which creates an even number of ends. You can just tie off and on again at the peg in this case. You'll have to pull the next single strand from the back through the reed to tie to the peg when you restart in this case

Lastly, if you find that crossing of threads at the back of your loom during the direct warp interferes with opening your shed, you can put a warp or pick-up stick in the back shed opening, p.20.

If you want to break down and buy a warping board to resolve extra length, odd number of ends, and crossing threads however, all of the books in my bibliography demonstrate its use. Warping boards can be helpful for preparing warp in advance when you don't want to tie up your loom.

With direct warping, warp length is the distance from the yarn on the apron rod to the back of the warping peg. I like to sling my tape measure from my table edge to the back of the peg to set up. When I use my Schacht Cricket loom, I measure 2 - 3" more than the warp length given in patterns. This is because the Cricket's apron rod extends forward from the table edge by a couple of inches. With some looms, you may not need to add any inches as their apron rod coincides with the table edge when clamped down.

When I ask for a 15" wide warp on a reed that allows exactly 15" weaving width, pull the first loop to the outside of the reed. When you sley the ends through the holes, one of those ends will be placed in the first hole to the left and one will stay on the outside. This way you use the entire 15". Take note of the weaving width of your reeds. My Cricket, 10 dent reed is actually 15-1/2" weaving width and my 5 dent is 15-1/4", so this outside loop requirement only applies to my 8 and 12 dent reeds in this book.

For wide warps, besides packing with warp sticks, you should always place your warp on to your apron rods inside (toward the center side of) the outer apron strings (or whatever attaches the apron rod to the loom). This way they won't sneak off the end of the rod to cause trouble. Flare your apron strings outward, if applicable, to protect the warp at each end.

17

Weaving a Header

It is assumed that you will always weave a header to spread the warp evenly before you start. Some weavers use tissue or plastic strips for this purpose. Others insist that you should use a yarn that is the weight of your weaving yarn to spread the warp accurately. I don't see a problem with either choice. Unless my yardage available is really limited, I just weave the header with my weaving yarn for convenience. If you are only beating your header every 2 or 3 picks, you won't waste much anyway because it will spread faster than beating every pick.

I like to place one strip of plastic in the shed after the header to differentiate the "good" weaving from the "junk" weaving (the header). This can be especially helpful when hemstitching (p.22) because you can easily pull that piece out to form a nice gap to lasso the warp threads with your stitch. I just roll up a kitchen garbage bag and cut it for all the strips I need.

If you end the header by placing the plastic piece in a down shed, you will be all ready to start in an up shed. This is how I begin my mantra to keep track of whether I changed the shed as I throw (especially handy when distracted). Whether you are right or left handed, if you start your first throw on the right in an up shed, you can repeat, "Up right, Down left." This is great for all the plain weave you will do. If you are about to throw on the right, your shed should be up, and conversely on left. This will be much faster than finding out you are in the wrong shed by unraveling. You may curse me when changing to a pick-up pattern or multiple shuttle handling because it will mess with your mantra, but the loss will only be temporary before you are back in rhythm with plain weave. Sticking your finger in an open shed to see if your last pick is locked in by the change of shed also works, but it's still slower.

Setting a Pick-up Stick for Patterns in this Book

For use in warp and weft floats featured in the Tweed Vest, p.78 and the Pillars and Hedgerows Scarf, p.90, here's the set up of your pick-up stick:

With down shed open, reach behind the reed and use the beveled edge of the stick to pick-up the 1st and every other thread of the top layer of warp only. These are the slot threads. Floats only work if you are engaging with slot threads. Once set, push the stick away from you to the back beam. It won't interfere with your work unless you pull it forward as instructed in the float rows.

Handling 2 Shuttles for 2 color weaving

When you are alternating colors as in the "Pillars and Hedgerows" scarf or the "Tweed Vest", at certain points, you will have 2 shuttles on the same side, and you will wonder how these yarns should wrap around each other as you throw.

I use a method for consistent wrapping of the weft yarns that I call **"the Under/Under - Over/Over"**, If the <u>weft</u> from the last pick thrown is sitting <u>under the outermost warp thread</u>, you take the next shuttle and wrap it <u>under the previous shuttle thread</u> before throwing. If the <u>weft</u> from the last pick thrown is sitting <u>over the outermost selvedge thread</u>, the next shuttle wraps its thread <u>over the thread of the previous shuttle</u> before throwing. This keeps the yarn from sinking into the shed and missing the outermost warp end. Once you get the hang of this, you can think less about your edge and weave more quickly.

My method for optimal selvedges

<u>Make the 2 outer selvedge threads on each side a little closer together than the interior warp threads, but don't pull so tightly that they tumble on top of each other and make unsightly ridges</u>. Here's how:

1. **Throw the shuttle** through the shed & pull the yarn through.

2. **Drop the shuttle** in your lap or on top of your fabric.

3. **Set the edge.** Place your finger just inside the open shed (see right) and push the edge to a point for our triangle coming in step 4.

4. **Set the triangle** rising in the direction of the throw. Let the yarn rise about 35°. May need 45° for worsted, less for lace, to allow for take up – experiment and practice.

5. **Place both hands on top of the reed & beat lightly.**

Take charge of edges to line them up (one above the other) somewhat snugly. Wimpy edges look mouse chewed when the tension is released. <u>Your weaving width will often draw-in about 10% as you work to get the optimal selvedge described at left. This can vary somewhat by fiber, yarn weight, or sett, so judge each fabric according to how your edges look.</u> Mohair, for example, barely draws in.

As you work, measure width often for consistent draw-in. After washing, there will likely be additional shrinkage.

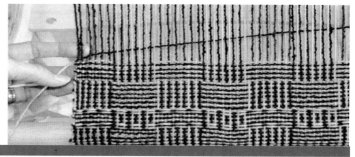

Troubleshooting

If you are using a warp yarn that has a lot of loose fiber, like mohair, OR if you have excessive crossing of threads in the back of the loom, you may find that your shed will not open cleanly. Insert a warp stick, a pick up stick, or an extra shuttle into the shed opening behind the loom, and push it all the way back to the rear beam. This will help you separate warp threads to keep an open shed. This can also help you sharpen up warp threads if some of them slacken in the weaving process. You can leave it there while weaving, or just push the threads open as needed, and remove it.

When weaving lighter weight fabrics, you might find it disturbing when the front tie-on bows roll under the fabric as you advance, creating bumps in the fabric and a wavy fell line. If this is more than minimal, you can use a paper towel core to cover the bows before they roll under. Just slice the core up the middle and snap it around the front rod and over the knots before they disappear – problem solved.

Here's a great tip that came from Holly in Boynton Beach, Fl, a new and creative weaver. If you just can't seem to avoid catching your loose weft yarn on the ratchet at right front as you throw your shuttle, place a foot sock over the ratchet handle or the entire right front corner if you prefer.

You may still catch your yarn on the mechanism occasionally, but it will untangle much faster using the sock.

..and what about

BROKEN WARP THREADS?!

I always promise my new weavers, that if they weave enough, they will eventually break a thread in process. Breaks happen. This is usually due to a knot or flaw in the yarn and nothing you did to make it happen. My repair kit consists of a small pill bottle with cap. Inside I have 5-6 pennies and a T pin.

Weave the T pin securely into the fabric near the edge with the head of the pin near the exit point of the broken warp thread. I wrap the front broken piece around the head a couple times, and trim the broken end at the back. Then I cut the replacement yarn to the length I need to finish plus 10%, plus another 12-18". This I tie to the same T pin head. I like to make a half knot, and then wrap this thread a of couple times around the pin head. Thread this replacement end where the broken end was supposed to go, hang it off the backside of the loom, and let it hang loose towards the floor using the pill bottle as a weight. You place the thread over the opening of the bottle, and snap the cap onto it to attach. The pill bottle will hang towards the floor. You won't even know it's there until the next time you move the loom aside and find it hanging there.

As you advance your fabric, you will occasionally need to move the weight downward. Don't remove the T pin until the weaving comes off the loom. Then you'll just pick out the knot, and needle weave one of the ends away from the other so they don't end in the same place. Cut ends after washing.

Finishing Edges with Fringe

My old advice was to cut the project off the back of the loom allowing for fringe, remove it from the front rod, and be very careful not to unravel edges as you remove the header and tie tassels –**YIKES!**

There's a better way. I compiled this from the advice of several of my beginning students. Nowadays, I start by cutting fringe for the ending edge by cutting only the threads I need as I tie each tassel into overhand knots. Before removing your project from the loom, use tape (cellophane, masking, repositionable…) to mark a cutting line for at least 6" of fringe at the end. Tassels can be cut shorter later, but less than 6" at this stage is hard to handle.

Cut just the strands you are tying in the first tassel (along the bottom edge of the tape line), and make a big overhand loop for the knot. Pull the loop up against the woven edge before pulling it tight. Repeat across. No unraveling here!

Now unroll the fabric, slide it off, or untie it from, the front apron rod, and tape this unfinished end to your work table, just above the starting edge. If you have not already done so, untie the bows and knots you used to tie on.

Next cut the weft (only) up the middle of the header to your starting edge (up to the plastic strip if you used one as a separator). Avoid cutting any warp fringe. You should lift your scissor point up so you can see that only the header weft is sitting on the blade as you cut. (Seriously, this is not scary if you make sure your scissor point emerges as you work.)

This cut makes it really easy to grab the header weft at each side about 1/2" in from each edge, and pull out 2 strands at a time up to the start of your weaving with no stress to the finished edge.

Now with the work still taped to the table, you can easily tie tassels across without causing the weaving to unravel –**YEAH!**

Need pictures?

Check out my YouTube Video, "A Simple Method to Remove Weaving from the Rigid Heddle Loom".

21

Hemstitching Fringed Edges

There are many right ways to hemstitch. Here's the way I do it:

At the beginning of weaving, allow a tail of weft that is 4 times the weaving width. Weave 1/2" or so.

Thread a tapestry needle with the weft tail that you left at the beginning. If you have put a piece of plastic between your header and your weaving, you can pull that out using your tapestry needle.

Start on the right, if you are right handed. Left handers may want to work from the left, and reverse the horizontal direction of each step, reversing the "L" formation you will create.

Decide on the number of warp ends you wish to bundle together. This is a matter of taste. Your needle will go over x warp threads and up x weft picks to pierce your fabric diagonally from back to front For our example, we will use 3 warp ends over and 2 picks up to bundle the 3 ends together.

You may wish to divide the number of total warp ends by the number of ends you are bundling to come out even at the left, although I don't feel it makes a noticeable difference if you have less ends in your last bundle.

Step 1

(Pierce the fabric edge diagonally.) From the right side, insert the needle from the back through the front of the fabric, finding the exit point that is over 3 warp strands and up 2 weft picks. Pull the sewing yarn through completely, keeping the needle from catching the loose thread in this step.

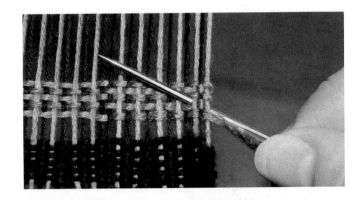

Step 2

(Lasso the warp threads.) Bring the needle back to the right, and use it to lift the first 3 strands of warp below the beginning edge of the weaving. Pull the loose sewing yarn downward and under the needle before you exit to catch the loose yarn, then pull the needle to the left.

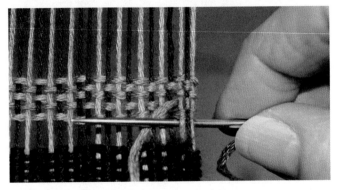

22

Tighten the resulting loop snugly to secure the warp strands surrounded. These 2 steps form a little "L" shape (A).

Repeat these 2 steps across. After the first time, step 1 will repeat at the place you left off, right next to the warp ends that are already surrounded. The needle will go under the fabric below the first pick and pierce forward from the back (B). Your step 2 will always start back at that point where you started step 1, surrounding the next 3 unbundled warp threads.

TO END: at the left selvedge, I improvise with the diagonal to pierce the fabric inside the outermost warp end on step 1, and then bundle the last warp strands. Secure the sewing yarn by creating a loop around the last warp thread and pull the needle through it to knot. Needle weave the sewing yarn into the fabric, away from the edge, and trim the tail after washing.

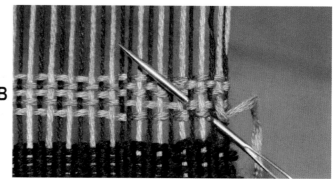

Ending Edge

Cut a weft tail at right that is 4 times your weaving width.

Step 1

Thread the tapestry needle with this end, and working from the back through the front of the piece, bring the needle through the fabric at 3 warp strands left and 2 weft picks <u>down</u>.

Step 2

Bring the needle back to the right, and lift the first 3 strands of warp <u>above</u> the fabric edge. This time, the loose sewing yarn will be pulled <u>up and under the needle</u> to catch the yarn and form an upside-down L shape. Tighten snugly to secure the warp bundle and work across to finish the left side the same as you did the lower edge.

It also works to end with the tail at the left, and turn your loom around so that the ending will work like the beginning edge.

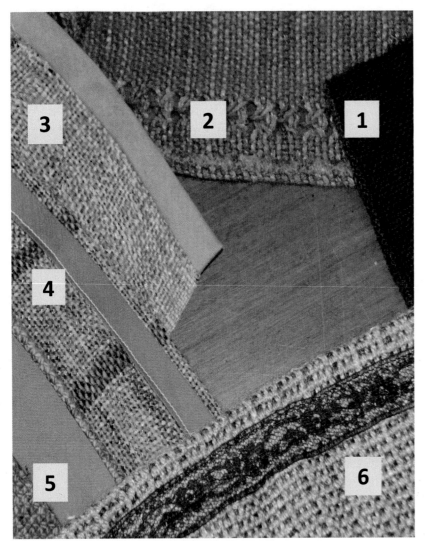

No Fringe Edges

Don't want fringe? Some weavers double fold the fabric to make a hem, but I find that too bulky for my taste. Here are my favorite ways to get rid of the fringe:

1. Raw Finish (It all starts here).

This is the least refined edge, but the least bulky for reversible ease. When you weave multiple pieces on one warp, weave 2 picks of scrap yarn in between each piece on your warp. Whether multiple or single pieces, your beginning and final edges will be protected from unraveling with a scrap header at the beginning and a 1/2" scrap header at the end.

STITCHING: I consider the weft pick at the very edge of a piece to be sacrificial in this process. Aim at zig zag stitching across to link together the 2nd and 3rd pick from the edge. After the first row, turn, and overlap another zig zag row just inside your first row.

Double zig zag is crucial for a secure edge. Trim close to your stitching. You can unravel that 1st pick, and If you accidentally caught it in your stitching, it will blend in.

Be careful with stretchy yarns like rayon as your edge can stretch and get a little wavy. The walking foot attachment will help.

Some weavers use sergers to great effect on a raw edge. You can also try an overcast edge stitch if your sewing machine allows. My aim is to demonstrate that sophisticated effects can be achieved with simple tools, but I'm not going to tool shame you if you wish to invest a little more!

If you have multiple pieces on 1 warp, be sure to stitch each edge before you cut those pieces apart.

2. Raw Hem. This one involves folding the raw finished edge approximately 3/8" to the wrong side, press, and machine stitch with a straight stitch just below the raw finish edge. The raw hem works well for a minimal, one sided edge on lightweight fabrics.

3. Encased Edge. This creates a more refined edge that is reversible. Using a coordinating double fold, bias seam binding, cut it the length of the raw finished edge plus 5/8" at each end. Open out one of the long folded edges of binding, match it to the right side of the raw edge of weaving, pin in place, and stitch the binding to the fabric as shown below. Fold the extra 5/8" allowed at each end inward (wrong sides of tape together) and press. Turn the other long folded edge over to the wrong side of weaving and hand stitch along this edge on the wrong side using a blind stitch. This means making one long stitch through the folded edge and one tiny stitch into the woven fabric making the stitch invisible. Sew both ends of the casing shut with a blind stitch as well.

4. Folded hem with encased edge. This is a tidy, one sided hem for a firmer edge. Follow #3 above, skipping the 2nd side blind stitching, turn the encased edge to the wrong side of your garment to hem to your desired length, press, and hand or machine stitch in place along the tape's center folded edge to secure. Where the hem meets any knitted edge, I whipstitch the side edge to the knitting to close gaps.

5. Folded hem with wide encased edge. Same as #4, but the center fold on the seam binding was opened and pressed flat for wider coverage and a more substantial hem. Stitch the other long folded edge to the wrong side by hand or machine stitching.

6. Lace seam binding. This is a nice, lightweight treatment for a folded hem. Just machine sew flexible lace seam binding over the top of the raw finish edge on the right side of fabric, turn the hem to wrong side, press, and blind stitch in place by hand or machine stitch.

Attach seam binding to a raw finish edge. I use *Wrights* bias tape, extra wide, double fold, .5 inch wide.

Finish & Seaming

Finishing

You <u>must wash your work before wearing</u>. This helps your fabric become its awesome self, easing gaps, puckers, and stiffness. I normally wash my woven pieces before adding stitches or sewing together for easier handling and calculated fit. I use a no-rinse, mild wash, purchased from my local yarn shop and recommended for hand made fabrics. Drop the piece(s) in sudsy, lukewarm water, agitate lightly to dampen throughout, and soak for at least 15 minutes. No rinse required, and it conditions the fabric. Wools can be treated to higher temps and squeezed to agitate further to full and stabilize the fabric if needed.

Squeeze excess water from the work. Don't wring as that would torque the fabric unduly You can roll it in a towel, and step on it to squeeze more water out if desired. I hang the pieces over a round towel rod or hanger to air dry. Square rods or wire hangers will leave unsightly dents in your fabric. When dry, yarn tails are trimmed flush.

I use a moderate steam setting for most of my fabrics as they are more prone to wrinkles and less likely to flatten than knitting. Be careful with your knitted elements. Check yarn labels for further cautions. Some knitted pieces, like bamboo, may need wet blocking rather than ironing.

Despite careful calculations, weaver's results vary due to weaving style and shrinkage of different yarns. <u>Measurements can only be approximations</u> for this reason. I strongly recommend that you <u>measure your pieces before sewing them together</u> to make sure you are getting the desired widths and lengths. When fit is important, you may be able to borrow or add to seam allowances or knitted side panels as applicable. If you have fabric length discrepancies, you can raw finish and trim the longer pieces to match.

The photo at right shows a top down view of 2 examples of my **sloped shoulder overlap.** I devised this method for designs that are enhanced by a sloped shoulder when the raw edges are at the top and bottom of the garment. See the diagram on p.27 to complete the following steps:

1. Complete the "encased edge" described on p.25 on upper raw edges.

2. Overlap the wrong side of the encased back shoulder edge at armhole over the right side of the front shoulder edge by the amount specified in the pattern (from 1" to 2").

3. Angle the 2 pieces away from each other towards the neck opening to create the shoulder length measurement given in the pattern. Pin in place.

4. On the right side, top stitch   as shown, close to the edge of seam binding and at armhole overlap to secure.

Overlap Seam

When sewing a traditional seam with an allowance of 3/8" - 5/8", I press that seam open. When I specify an overlap seam as in the Watercolor Kimono, p.66, I place the selvedge of 1 piece on top of the selvedge of the other, overlapping by a specified amount, and pin in place. Since these pieces have a tendency to slip out of place in process, I hand baste them together before machine stitching close to the edge. Sometimes I stitch again 1/4" away.

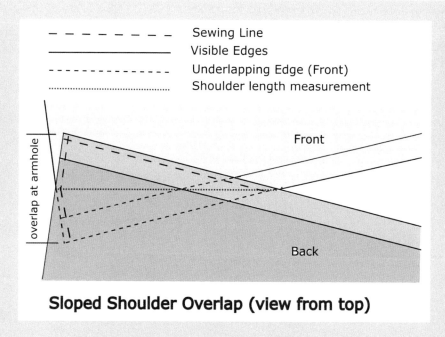

– – – – – – –	Sewing Line
———————	Visible Edges
- - - - - - - - -	Underlapping Edge (Front)
....	Shoulder length measurement

overlap at armhole

Front

Back

Sloped Shoulder Overlap (view from top)

Note that when you overlap the pieces on an angle like this, the armhole edge won't line up perfectly. Topstitch through all thickness as shown. This unevenness will be hidden in the seam allowance or covered by the crochet trim per pattern.

Knitting Advice

#1

#2

Fastest Way to Pick Up Stitches to Knit

My long trail of addiction to fiber craft led to weaving as a way to get my knitting fix and speed up results, so I pick up a lot of stitches along woven selvedges. Start with a crochet hook, like one of these pictured above, with no added handle. Pulling knit stitches with a hook puts less stress on the woven edge than gouging into the fabric with the knitting needle looking for a stitch.

Working on the right side of the fabric, use the hook to pick up 10-20 stitches, (A) then slide them off the opposite end of the hook onto the knitting needle (B). Always do this on a selvedge edge or a folded hemmed edge (not along a raw edge which is too vulnerable). Pick up your stitches 2 picks below the edge.

If you happen to have an Addi Turbo Click crochet hook, #2 at left, you can poke your needle into the open tube end of the hook (B), and slide the stitches easily onto your needle. If using a hook like #1, just scoop the stitches off the backside onto the needle.

ALSO...

Sometimes I mark off even intervals along the edge with locking stitch markers. Then I divide the total number of stiches I need to pick up by the number of intervals. This way I can check at each marker that I am getting my stitch count.

I often get my count by inserting the hook about every 2 picks of weaving. If you are off by 1 or 2 stiches at the end, it generally doesn't matter for the knitted side panels herein. If you are off substantially, or for a lace or rib pattern, back up and retry, or find a gap where you can pull up an extra stitch from the knitting yarn that travels along the wrong side.

It does not work well to try to increase in a stitch on your first row across, in case you are tempted. Tried that, and can tell you that it will show up badly!

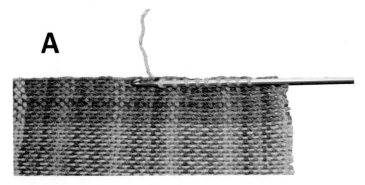

A

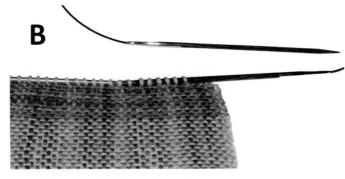

B

It is beyond the scope of this book to convey basic knitting, crochet, or sewing skills. If you need more support on these, classes from your local yarn shop, *www.Youtube.com, www.Wikihow.com,* and *www.Craftsy.com* are just some of the excellent resources available. Backwards loop cast on, blind stitch hemming, magic loop knitting, and other simple skills used here can be searched online if you don't already know them.

There are two unique and useful methods I will describe below. A video of "Grandma's Favorite Bind Off" can be found on the website of Michelle Hunter, *www.knitpurlhunter*.com. She and her website are delightful, by the way. Also, I use German Short Rows extensively for shaping. Several videos of this effective short row method can be found on *Youtube.com.*

Grandma's Favorite Bind Off: my favorite bind off when a very relaxed edge is needed.

1. Purl 2 sts together, wrapping them clockwise. Complete the p2tog.

2. Slide the new stitch created from the right hand needle to the left hand needle.

Repeat steps 1 and 2 until 1 stitch is left. Cut the yarn, pass it through the last stich, and pull snug.

German Short Rows: a short row method that minimizes gapping at the turn of the row. It helps to have 2 markers or safety pins for each repeat. I'll admit that I don't use markers because I am used to the appearance of the double stitch, but you may want them.

Work across in pattern up to the turning point given, turn your work, and if the working yarn is not already in front of you, pull it to the front between needles. Slip the last, left hand stitch to the right hand needle, and place a marker or pin on right hand needle.

Lift the working yarn up (tugging the st from the row below upward), and bring the yarn around the back side of the right hand needle. This lifts the stitch below upward, to make a double stitch showing on front, a twist at the top of the needle, and a double stitch on the back side formed by the working yarn. Continue to work back across the row up to the turning point (defined by pattern) at the other end. Turn your work, repeat the double stitch effect at this end, and place a marker.

These 2 rows are 1 repeat. Each time you repeat, you will stop at the designated number of stitches from the marker or double stitch. When all repeats are done, a final row will be worked treating all double stitches created as one stitch.

The Palindrome Warp

A palindrome is a word, phrase, sentence, or number that reads the same forward as backward (example: RADAR). A palindrome warp will maximize the beauty of a hand dyed skein by laying out blocks of color in the same areas. Although I did not invent it, as a color fiend, I love the palindrome warp!

Choosing Yarn: For warp, this technique requires skeins that are dyed in a symmetrical fashion like this…

…where one side of the skein matches the other side with a pivot point at each end. You will have to turn the skein until you find its pivot points. It helps to jot down a description of the pivot point colors, before your skein gets wound into a ball. Not all hand dyed yarn is created this way, so be sure to inspect the layout of the color when you select your yarn. Your weft yarn should be a solid or tonal yarn that picks up one of the colors of the warp. A darker tone will make the colors sing.

Warp length, for a palindrome project, is calculated in multiples of the skein length stretched taut. This length must be enough for your project, but may need to be greater than what is needed in order to come out in multiples of the skein length.

Example: Start with the skein length. Let's assume it is 34" stretched. If your project requires a warp of 56", you will still need a length of 68" because that is 2 times the skein length. In this case there is a little unavoidable waste, a casualty of this process.

When ready to warp, your beautiful skein will have been wound in to a ball. Lay out a strand from the balled up yarn ,and maneuver the strand until you find the 2 pivot points that allow colors to match forward and back, about 34" apart. Tie the center of the first pivot point around the apron rod, and cut away the excess strand before that point.

Once you drag your first loop to the peg, run your hand along the strand as you walk back to the loom. Adjust the table position and yarn tension to make the return strand colors lay alongside those of the forward strand. As you continue, watch that the colors pool in the same general area this way. You are not trying for an exact striping of color. A blend of color between the stripes is the goal. You may have to pull some loops tighter than others as you work across to make this happen.

When you get the length adjusted right, you should be able to proceed quickly. If the yarn starts giving you more than minimal trouble about lining up as you work across, it is ok to cut the yarn and restart it to get the color pooling back in sync. You'll have to locate the right pivot point again if you do this. Plain weave with a solid or tonal weft yarn.

SUMMER TOPS

Linen Lace Tunic

Equipment

- 8 dent reed
- Warp sticks for wider warp (if desired, p.9)
- 15" pick-up stick
- F crochet hook
- Sewing machine
- Straight pins

Materials

- Interlacements Irish Linen for warp, 1 skein Reds Plus
- Blue Heron Silk Linen for weft, 1 skein Cardinal
- Sewing thread

Skills Added

Lightweight and airy, this is the perfect spring top. Grab your sewing machine and you'll have this one together in no time at all. A 2:2 leno weave with the use of a pick-up stick creates the lace yoke. One long warp around 14' takes care of all six pieces needed.

I've built an average of 4-6" of ease into this loose fitting tunic. I found that shrinkage in length and width is about 13% with these yarns after washing.

Weaving gauge	8 epi, 13 ppi for plain weave, 6 ppi for leno weave.			
To Fit Bust Sizes	32-34"	36-38"	40-42"	44-46"
Finished Measurement at Bust	39"	42"	46"	49"
Finished Length (from shoulder at neck to bottom edge)	27"	28"	29"	29-3/4"
Warp yardage	432	479	528	573
Weft yardage	481	538	602	650
Warp Length	162"	166"	170"	172"
Warp Width in Loom	12 "	13"	14"	15"
# Warp Ends	96	104	112	120
Weaving Length ea. (body piece, make 4)	22"	23"	23-1/2"	24"
(yoke piece, make 2)	25"	25"	25"	26"

To Warp With Irish Linen, prepare warp for size given above. Wind shuttle with Silk Linen

Weaving Instructions

BODY PIECES (Weave 4): With the Silk Linen as weft, weave 1-1/2" plain weave, weave 1 repeat of 2:2 leno (see pages 34-35), then complete piece to length for your size. Separate multiple pieces with 2 picks of scrap yarn. Weave a 1/2" ending header when complete, remove from loom, and finish top and bottom edges of each piece according to raw finish (p.24).

YOKE PIECES (Weave 2): With Silk Linen, weave 14 picks of plain weave and complete 1 repeat of 2:2 leno. *Weave 4 picks plain weave and complete 1 repeat of 2:2 leno. Repeat from * until 1" less than weaving length for yoke sizes above. End with 13 picks of plain weave, weave 2 picks of scrap yarn between pieces, finish with a 1/2" header of scrap yarn . Raw finish top and bottom edges of both pieces.

Cut pieces apart, hand wash (p. 26), and hang or dry flat. Sew garment together according to step-by-step instructions on pages 36 - 37, being careful to check measurements for your size. Slight adjustments can be made by adding to, or subtracting from, seam allowances.

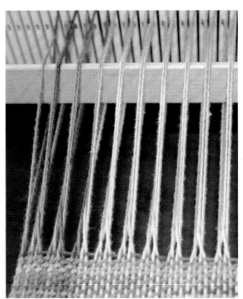

Step 1

Start with an open shed. <u>Shuttle can end on either side as long as the right, outermost warp end is in the up position.</u> Weave another pick if needed to make this happen. Pull top row ends to left to pick up 2 ends on lower row. Place those on top of the stick. Let 2 ends from top row snap under the pick-up stick.

Step 2

Repeat Step 1 across. This will bring up and twist 2 lower threads from the bottom row with 2 threads of the upper row each time. <u>Check frequently to see that your twists look the same all the way across. If they don't, back up and correct. Also see *</u> <u>below.</u>

Step 3

Push the pick-up stick away from you and turn it upright on its edge to open a special shed.

Advice on Leno Weave

Leno can also be worked with 1 thread on top crossing with 1 thread on the bottom. That would be 1:1 leno.

*This weave can be frustrating if you find that your threads are not twisting the same throughout. You start over and still can't get all the twists to look the same. Meanwhile, it may seem like the warp ends blur together. Most weavers new to leno have an ah ha! moment once they can clearly see the part where <u>the hovering threads of the top row of warp must travel from the right of the pick up threads on the bottom row, all the way to the left of those threads every time.</u> This is why that right outermost thread must be up to start (makes a tight cross). If you notice that the top row threads you are pushing left are already positioned to the left of the targeted threads on bottom, you have skipped a warp thread. This awareness will make this weave easy.

Sometimes you will do the 2:2 leno and find that you only have 1:1 left to twist together at the very end of the row. See my example at the right. I don't find this particularly bothersome. Edges will not be perfect anyway because you have to ease the weft up at the sides to accommodate the 1/2" rise. As careful as you might be, this weave tends to suck the edges inward, so don't get hung up on perfection. Your best results will be obtained if you are conscientious about leaving the edges loose, but not sloppy, for the 2 rows of the leno repeat.

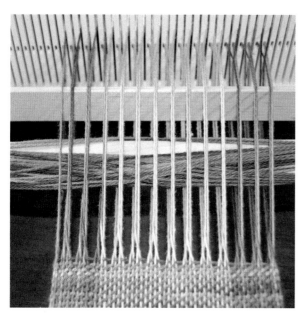

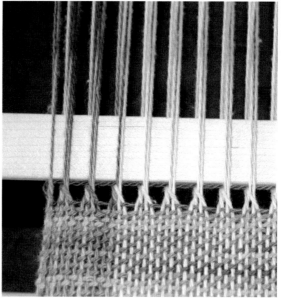

Step 4

Throw the shuttle through the special shed in front of the pick-up stick.

Step 5

Flatten the pick-up stick, and use it to push this new pick into place about 1/2" above the fabric edge. Adjust your selvedge so it is loose, but neat. Remove the stick.

Final Step (2nd Pick)

Change the shed (a must to lock in the twist) and throw another pick. When you use the reed to "beat" this pick into place, you are actually just placing that 2nd pick to rise the same amount as the first pick. Yes, you must resist the urge to beat that 2nd pick down once your grab the reed. You should see 2 even gaps with each repeat of this weave.

For visual instruction on this weave, go to the video page of *www.poffstudio.com* for "Leno on Rigid Heddle" or follow Poff Studio at *www.youtube.com*.

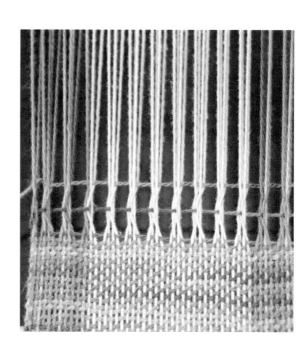

2:2 Leno Weave

35

Sewing it Together

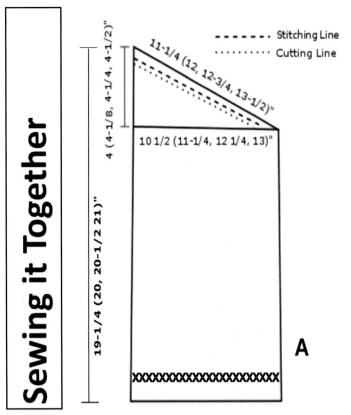

Legend:
- - - - - Stitching Line
.... Cutting Line

11-1/4 (12, 12-3/4, 13-1/2)"

4 (4-1/8, 4-1/4, 4-1/2)"

10 1/2 (11-1/4, 12 1/4, 13)"

19-1/4 (20, 20-1/2 21)"

A

Preparing 4 Body Pieces (measurements after washing, before hemming)

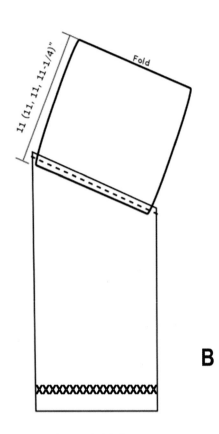

Fold

11 (11, 11, 11-1/4)"

B

Attach Yoke

Step 1

Fold top edge of each Body piece diagonally to the dimensions above in A. Pin in place, iron along the diagonal, and stitch 1/4" away from this edge. Cut away the excess fabric, close to stitching as shown. The side with the raw edge showing on the diagonal edge will be the right side of the fabric. BE SURE TO PREPARE 2 PIECES THAT SLOPE TO THE RIGHT AND 2 THAT SLOPE TO THE LEFT SO THEY CAN MATCH UP AS SHOWN IN C.

Step 2

On each raw finish end of both Yoke pieces, turn a 3/8" hem to wrong side, press and machine stitch in place.

Step 3

Take one hemmed end of a Yoke piece and place its WS over the RS of one Body piece (B). We'll call this a left front piece. Overlap the Yoke to cover the raw hem of the Body piece, centering yoke along the diagonal edge. This will leave approximately 3/8" excess at each edge on Body piece for later seaming. Pin in place, hand baste this edge as it may shift during stitching. Machine stitch through all thicknesses close to Yoke edge and 1/4" away.

To this same yoke piece, attach a left back Body piece as you did with front piece, being careful to match the direction of the slope, front and back. Repeat this for the right half.

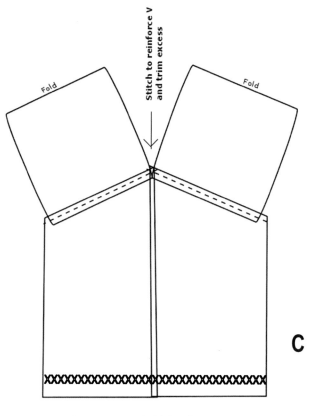

Center and Side Seams

C

Step 4

Overlap the selvedges of 2 Body pieces at center per diagram C allowing 3/8" overlap. Pin in place and hand baste. Machine stitch through all thicknesses close to selvedge and 1/4" away.

Complete the other side in the same fashion.

Step 5

Machine stitch in the V of front and back neck openings through the overlapping seam allowance using 2 rows of straight stitch, close to the Yoke edge to reinforce, and trim away the excess fabric close to this stitching. Crochet finish later will finesse this V.

With wrong sides of Body pieces together, stitch side seams with a 3/8" seam allowance and press open.

Finish

Turn a 3/8" hem at bottom edge and press. Complete hem according to raw hem, p.24, #2.

CROCHET: With size F crochet hook, attach Silk Linen at back neck opening at the 8th leno repeat above the back V. Sc around entire neck opening to starting point, covering any raw edges at V's. Ch 5 (5-1/4, 5-3/4, 6-1/4)" to make the back bridge, and attach at other back yoke piece (at same height above back V). Work 4 (or desired number) rows of sc across bridge and weave in crochet ends.

East Meets West Blouse

Equipment

- 12 dent reed
- G Crochet Hook for sleeves OR US 5, 32" circular knitting needles for knitted sleeves
- Warp sticks for wider warp (if desired, p.9)
- Sewing machine
- Sewing Needle
- Straight pins

Materials

- Hamilton Yarns Heaven's Hand Shaman, 2 (2, 2, 2, 2, 2, 2, 3) skeins Lover
- Interlacements Zig Zag, 1 skein Mountain Jewel
- 3-1/2 yards of double fold bias seam binding
- 5 large metal snaps
- 5 Decorative Buttons to cover snaps
- Sewing thread

Skills Added

Comfort and drape characterize this shapely, snap front blouse. Yes, snap! The buttons are just a cover up.

Accented by a trendy high-low hem, side slits and a contrast yoke, this rayon and raw silk combination is easy to wear. Warp 10 ends and skip a heddle to add a little vertical texture to the weave. Close fitting with 1-2" of ease, this one finishes with a basic half double crochet around the armholes for a short sleeve. **Knitted sleeve variation offered at the end.**

Weaving gauge:	Using a 12 dent reed, you will thread 10 epi by skipping 1 heddle in each inch.							
	12 ppi for Zig Zag and 14ppi for Shaman.							
To Fit Bust Sizes	30"	32"	34"	36"	38"	40"	42"	44"
Finished Measurement at Bust	31"	33"	35"	37"	39"	41"	43"	45"
Finished Length (from shoulder at neck to bottom front edge. Back hangs approx. 1" longer)	22-1/2"	22-1/2"	23"	23"	23-1/2"	23-1/2"	24"	24"
Shaman yardage	464	483	519	547	585	622	654	682
Zig Zag yardage	301	315	336	355	374	396	415	430
Warp Length	130"	130"	132"	132"	134"	134"	136"	136"
Warp Width in Loom	10-1/2"	11"	11-1/2"	12-1/4"	12-3/4"	13-1/2"	14"	14-1/2"
# Warp Ends	106	110	116	122	128	136	140	146
Weaving Length (front, make 2)	26"	26"	26-1/2"	26-1/2"	27"	27"	27-1/2"	27-1/2"
Weaving Length (back, make2)	27"	27"	27-1/2"	27-1/2"	28"	28"	28-1/2"	28-1/2"

To Warp

With Shaman, warp your loom by sleying 10 ends (5 loops during direct warping), then skipping 1 slot and 1 hole in each inch. Working with width given for your size, you will end with 6 (10, 6, 2, 8, 6,10, 6) ends after the last skipped hole.

Weaving Instructions

For 2 front pieces, (starting edge of each piece will be bottom edge of garment) use Zig Zag to weave 21 (21, 21-1/4, 21-1/4, 21-1/2, 21-1/2, 21-3/4, 21-3/4)". Then with Shaman, weave 5 (5, 5-1/4, 5-1/4, 5-1/2, 5-1/2, 5-3/4, 5-3/4)". Separate the 2 pieces on 1 warp with 2 picks of scrap yarn and finish with a 1/2" ending header.

For 2 back pieces use Zig Zag to weave 22 (22, 22-1/4, 22-1/4, 22-1/2, 22-1/2, 22-3/4, 22-3/4)". Then with Shaman weave 5 (5, 5-1/4, 5-1/4, 5-1/2, 5-1/2, 5-3/4, 5-3/4)". Separate the pieces, and finish with an ending header as above.

See p.24 to complete raw finish edges. Cut pieces apart, wash (p.26), and hang dry.

Sew it Together

DARTS ON FRONT PIECES: (Diagram p.41) For each front piece, fold right side of fabric together matching the selvedges. Measure 14-1/2 (14-1/2, 14-3/4, 14-3/4, 15, 15, 15-1/4, 15-1/4)" down from top edge and place a pin to mark. Place another pin 2-1/2" further down. Sew 1/2" in from folded edge between these pins to complete darts.

Press the fold toward side selvedge.

CENTER BACK SEAM: Checking to see if pieces conform to desired measurements for your size, overlap center back pieces (right side over left) by 1-1/4", baste pieces together by hand, and top stitch them together close to the edge of the right side piece and then again 1" away.

Adjustments can be made by adding to or subtracting from seam allowances.

ENCASE TOP EDGES across back and fronts, p. 25 (#3), tuck in the center front ends, but do not tuck in the armhole ends of seam binding (all pieces). Trim it close to the armhole edge instead. Attach the seam binding on all bottom edges, press open for wide encased hem, p.25 (#5), but leave the sides and long edges unhemmed for now.

front pieces measurements after washing (back pieces are 1" longer)

23-1/4 (23-1/4, 23-3/4, 23-3/4, 24-1/4, 24-1/4, 24-3/4, 24-3/4)"

9 (9-1/2, 10, 10-1/2, 11,11-1/2, 12, 12-1/2)"

Darts on fronts add shape and are easy to make. Just fold the fabric in half at selvedges, locate the start for your size, and sew a 2-1/2" line, 1/2" inward as shown at right.

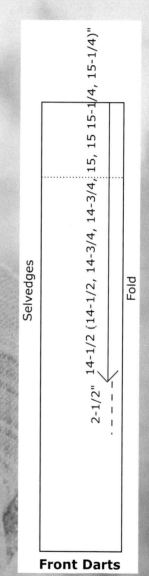

Selvedges

Fold

2-1/2" 14-1/2 (14-1/2, 14-3/4, 14-3/4, 15, 15 15-1/4, 15-1/4)"

Front Darts

41

SHOULDERS: See pages 26-27 to complete a sloped shoulder overlap, back pieces over fronts, for both shoulders. Your overlap will be 2 (2, 2, 2-1/4, 2-1/4, 2-1/4, 2-1/2, 2-1/2)" at shoulder edge and your shoulder length will be 4-1/2 (4-3/4, 5-1/4, 5-1/2, 5-3/4, 6, 6-1/4, 6-1/4)".

INTERFACINGS: Cut seam binding for interfacing to reinforce both front selvedges, open it at the center fold, and press flat. The cut length will need to reach from 1/2" above the bottom raw edge up to 7 (7-1/4, 7-1/2, 7-3/4, 8, 8-1/4, 8-1/4, 8-1/4)" below top edge of fronts PLUS 5/8". Turn this 5/8" to wrong side to finish one edge and press. Place WS finished edge down at top point, pin in place just 2 picks inward from selvedge. Baste and machine stitch according to diagram, starting in top right corner and following arrows.

SIDE SEAMS: Fold right sides together at shoulder, and measure down for armhole opening, 7 (7-1/2, 8, 8-1/2, 9, 9-1/2, 10, 10)". From underarm, pin fronts to back at sides. Back piece will be approximately 1" longer. With a 5/8" seam allowance, sew from underarm point toward the bottom edge, stopping 3-1/2" from bottom fronts to allow for side vents.

Press this seam open. Press armhole edge and side vents inward 5/8" to match. Top stitch 3/8" around armhole opening (squaring off at underarm). See diagram p.43.

HEMS: On fronts, bottom edges, fold the 5/8" allowed at each end of seam binding to WS and press, Close hem and blind stitch along sides and top of seam binding. Hem in same fashion. Machine top stitch 3/8" inward along side vents, 2nd diagram p.43.

SNAPS: On right front side, sew male piece of snap to interfacing starting just below top edge. Attach the 5 snap pieces evenly down to about 3" from bottom hemmed edge.

42

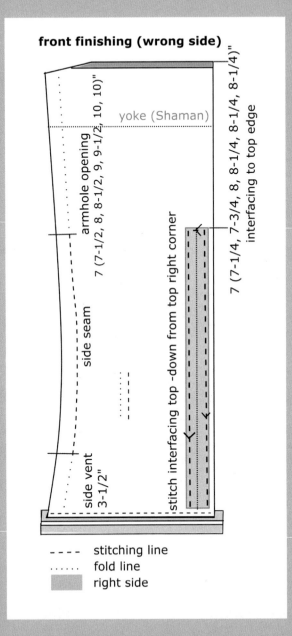

front finishing (wrong side)

yoke (Shaman)

armhole opening
7 (7-1/2, 8, 8-1/2, 9, 9-1/2, 10, 10)"

7 (7-1/4, 7-3/4, 8, 8-1/4, 8-1/4, 8-1/4)"
interfacing to top edge

side seam

stitch interfacing top -down from top right corner

side vent
3-1/2"

- - - - stitching line
. . . . . . fold line
▓▓▓ right side

On left front side attach the female pieces of snap to RS of garment to match other side. Sew buttons securely to RS of right front over location of snaps.

Crochet Sleeve

Hdc around sleeve opening for 15 rnds. Weave in ends.

Knitted Sleeve Option

Starting at underarm pick up 44 sts up one side and 44 sts down the other, p.28. Pm and work in garter stitch (knit 1 row, purl 1 row in the round) for 16 rows. It will be helpful to use your circular needles in a magic loop fashion (videos at *YouTube.com*) to get around the armhole.

Bind off loosely with Grandma's favorite bind off, p.29.

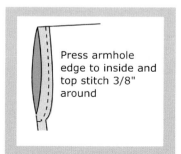

Press armhole edge to inside and top stitch 3/8" around

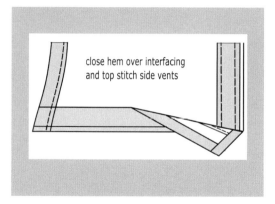

close hem over interfacing and top stitch side vents

Sleeveless Boat Neck Top

Equipment

- 10 dent reed
- 18-20 warp sticks (if desired for wider warp, p.9)
- US 4, 24" or 32" circular knitting needles,
- E or F crochet hook to pick up stitches and optional edge finish
- Stitch Markers
- Tapestry needle to finish ends
- Sewing machine
- Sewing needle

Materials

- Blue Heron Organic Cotton for main color, 1 skein Rosewood, and 1 skein Curry for contrast
- 2 yards double fold bias seam binding
- Sewing thread

Skills Added

This simple top has a retro appeal with a zero to negative ease (see Fit, p. 15). With the very close fit (made comfortable by stretchy side panels), you will want to use a soft smooth yarn. Blue Heron Organic Cotton is an ideal choice. Weave 2 pieces on the same warp, then pick up stitches to knit along the side edges and to shape armholes. **See an alternate option for curvier figures on the next page - a slightly longer version with side vents.**

Weaving gauge	10 epi, 9 ppi					
Knitting gauge	20 sts/ 38 rows over 4" in garter stitch (knit all rows)					
Finished Bust Measurement	34"	36"	38"	40"	42"	44"
Finished Length	20"	21"	21-1/2"	22"	22-1/2"	23"
Main Warp yds	369	392	413	439	461	468
Contrast Color yds	308	323	336	392	423	465
Warp Length	**72"**	**73"**	**74"**	**75"**	**76"**	**77"**
Warp Width in Loom	**13"**	**13-1/2"**	**14"**	**14-1/2"**	**15"**	**15"**
# Warp Ends	**130**	**134**	**138**	**146**	**150**	**150**
Weaving Length each (weave 2)	23-1/2"	24-1/2"	25"	25-1/2"	26"	26-1/2"

To Warp, Warp Order (see Chart Reading, p.16)

		4x			4x			4x		
Main Color	16 (18, 20, 24, 26,26)	2		22	2		22	2		16 (18, 20, 24, 26,26)
Contrast			2	2		2	2		2	2	

Weaving Instructions

Weaving with main color throughout, complete 2 identical pieces to length for your size. Separate multiple pieces with 2 picks of scrap yarn, and weave a 1/2" ending header of scrap yarn (see page 24 for raw finish). Wash and hang dry or dry flat before continuing, p.26.

Knitting Instructions

For both front and back pieces:

On RS, with contrast yarn, starting 1/2" from raw edge along selvedge, pick up 102 (105, 107, 110, 112,115) sts knit wise ending 1/2" from other raw edge (p.28). Knit in garter stitch (knit all rows) for 11 (12, 13, 14, 15, 17) rows. Bind off 37 (40, 42, 45, 47, 50) sts somewhat loosely for armhole and continue to end of row. Work 15 (16, 17, 18, 19, 22) more rows for a total of 27 (29, 31, 33, 35, 40) rows before binding off remaining sts somewhat loosely.

On opposite long edge, pick up same number of sts, 1/2 " in from both raw finished edges. On this edge you knit 10 (11, 12, 13, 14, 16) rows before binding off 37 (40, 42, 45, 47, 50) sts for armhole. Work to end of row. Complete 16 (17, 18 19, 20, 23) more rows on remaining sts, total 27 (29, 31, 33, 35, 40) rows, and bind off remaining sts.

Finishing

Finish top and bottom edges of weaving, level with knitted side panels, using folded hem with encased edge, p.25, #4. With contrast color, hand stitch front and back together at shoulder edges leaving a neck opening of 10-1/2 (11, 11-1/2, 12, 12-1/2, 12-1/2") and hand sew side seams together.

Armhole Finishing

Around armholes, starting at underarm, pick up 38 (40, 43, 45, 48, 50) sts on both front and back edges-total 76 (80, 86, 90, 96, 100) sts. Place marker at beginning of round. Knit 1 round. It will be helpful to use your circular needles in a Magic Loop fashion (videos at *YouTube.com*) to get around the armhole.

Begin German short rows as follows: (see p.29) Knit 1 round up to 3 sts before marker, turn work and complete short row double st. Knit back around up to 3 stitches before marker from other side, turn and repeat double stitch. This completes 1 repeat. You may wish to place a safety pin or marker at each double stitch to identify it more easily.

Complete this sequence 3 more times (4 total repeats). Each time, you will knit up to 3 sts before the last double stitch. Place marker after the last double stitch completed. Knit 1 complete round from here treating each double stitch as 1 st as they appear. Purl 1 additional round and then bind off.

Sc across the bottom of knitted side panels to finish (optional). Weave in knitting and crochet ends.

Measurements are after washing and hemming, before sleeve finish. Sleeve finishing will draw armhole height down about 1-1/2".

11-1/2 (12, 12-1/2, 13, 13-1/2, 13-1/2)"

2-3/4 (3, 3-1/4, 3-1/2, 3-3/4, 4-1/4)"

7-1/2 (8, 8-1/2, 9, 9-1/2, 10)"
Before armhole finish

13"

17 (18, 19, 20, 21, 22)"

Boat Neck Top
Variation with Side Vent

For curvier figures, this version adds 1" to length plus side openings to accommodate. Changes to pattern are shown at right.

Variation at left uses Blue Heron Organic Cotton, 1 skein Deep Blue Sea for main color and 1 skein Storm Cloud for contrast

Weaving gauge	10 epi, 9 ppi					
Knitting gauge	20 sts/ 38 rows over 4" in garter stitch (knit all rows)					
Finished Bust Measurement	34"	36"	38"	40"	42"	44"
Finished Length	21"	22"	22-1/2"	23"	23-1/2"	24"
Main Color yds.	390	414	436	463	487	494
Contrast Color yds.	325	341	355	414	447	491
Warp Length	74"	75"	76"	77"	78"	79"
Warp Width in Loom	**13"**	**13-1/2"**	**14"**	**14-1/2"**	**15"**	**15"**
# Warp Ends	**130**	**134**	**138**	**146**	**150**	**150**
Weaving Length (weave 2)	24-1/2"	25-1/2"	26"	26-1/2"	27"	27-1/2"

Instruction are the same as the original version except for blue highlighted items **and ...**

...Knitting Instructions

(for both woven pieces) On RS, with contrast yarn, starting 1/2" from raw edge along selvedge, pick up 107 (110, 112, 115, 117,120) sts knit wise ending 1/2" from other raw edge (p.28). Knit in garter stitch (knit all rows) for 11 (12, 13, 14, 15, 17) rows. Bind off 37 (40, 42, 45, 47, 50) sts somewhat loosely for armhole and continue to end of row. Work 15 (16, 17, 18, 19, 22) more rows for a total of 27 (29, 31, 33, 35, 40) rows before binding off remaining sts somewhat loosely.

On opposite long edge, pick up same number of sts, 1/2 " in from raw finished edges. On this edge you knit 10 (11, 12, 13, 14, 16) before binding off 37 (40, 42, 45, 47, 50) sts for armhole. Work to end of row. Complete 16 (17, 18 19, 20, 23) more rows on remaining sts, total 27 (29, 31, 33, 35, 40) rows, and bind off remaining sts. Work armhole finishing same as shorter version.

When sewing side seams together, leave 3" open at the bottom for the side vent.

Sc across the bottom of knitted side panels and around side vents to finish (optional). Weave in knitting and crochet ends.

Boatneck Top with Sleeves

Equipment

- 10 dent reed

- Warp sticks for wider warp (if desired, p.9)

- US 3 and 5, 24" or 32" circular knitting needles,

- E or F crochet hook to pick up stitches

- Tapestry needle to finish ends

- Sewing machine

- Sewing needle

Materials

- Interlacements Cabled Cotton for main color, 2 skeins Browntowne

- Interlacements Zig Zag for side panel and weft, 1 (1, 1, 1, 2, 2) skeins Cocoa

- Be Sweet Bamboo for sleeves, 4 (4, 4, 5, 5, 5) skeins #656 Chocolate

- 2 yards double fold bias tape

- Sewing thread

Skills Added

To me, a "fun to make" design involves just the right amount of variety and repetition. With that in mind, let's take the Boat Neck Top to new heights by adding texture with warp floats in the body and a lacy stitch in the knitted sleeves.

With my main concern still choosing soft fabrics for this close fit, the hand dyed Bamboo from Be Sweet used in these 3/4 sleeves is tonal luxury. Knitting skills are intermediate this time due to shaping and yarn overs in the sleeves.

Weaving gauge	10 epi, 10 ppi					
Knitting gauge	19 sts/ 40 rows over 4" in stockinette st using Zig Zag on US 5,					
	25 sts/ 32 rows over 4" in pattern stitch using Bamboo on US 5					
Finished Bust Measurement	34"	36"	38"	40"	42"	44"
Finished Length	20"	21"	21-1/2"	22"	22-1/2"	23"
Main Warp yds -Cabled Cotton	216	227	238	254	266	270
Sleeve & Contrast Warp yds -Bamboo	377	409	440	473	508	546
Side Panel and Weft yds.-Zig Zag	389	429	462	499	541	575
Warp Length	**72"**	**73"**	**74"**	**75"**	**76"**	**77"**
Warp Width in Loom	**13"**	**13-1/2"**	**14"**	**14-1/2"**	**15"**	**15"**
# Warp Ends	**130**	**134**	**138**	**146**	**150**	**150**
Weaving Length each (weave 2)	23-1/2"	24-1/2"	25"	25-1/2"	26"	26-1/2"

To Warp, Warp Order (see Chart Reading, p.16)

		4x			4x			4x		
Main Color	16 (18, 20, 24, 26,26)	2	22		2	22		2		16 (18, 20, 24, 26,26)
Contrast			2	2	2	2	2	2	2	

Weaving Instructions

Weaving with Zig Zag throughout, complete 2 identical pieces to length for your size. Separate multiple pieces with 2 picks of scrap yarn, and weave a 1/2" header of scrap yarn at the end. Prepare top and bottom edges of each piece according to raw finish, p.24. Wash and hang dry or dry flat before continuing, p.26.

Knitting Instructions

(both pieces) On RS, with Zig Zag yarn, starting 1/2" from raw edge along selvedge, pick up 96 (99, 102, 105, 108) sts knit wise ending 1/2" from other raw edge (see p.28). Knit in stockinette stitch (purl WS rows, knit RS rows) for 11 (12, 13, 14, 15, 17) rows. Bind off 31 (33, 35, 38, 40, 42) sts somewhat loosely for armhole and continue to end of row. Work 16 (17, 18, 19, 20, 23) more rows for a total of 28 (30, 32, 34, 36, 41) rows from cast on edge. AT THE SAME TIME, after initial bind off, ssk at each armhole edge to form underarm curve 4 (4, 4, 5, 5, 6) times. Continue straight until row count is complete, and bind off remaining sts somewhat loosely.

On opposite long edge, pick up same number of sts, 1/2" in from raw finished edges. On this edge, knit 10 (11, 12, 13, 14, 16) rows before binding off 31 (33, 35, 38, 40, 42) sts for armhole. Work to end of row. Complete 17 (18, 19, 20, 21, 24) more rows on remaining sts, total 28 (30, 32, 34, 36, 41) rows, decreasing with ssk at each armhole edge to curve underarm 4 (4, 4, 5, 5, 6) times. Bind off remaining sts somewhat loosely.

Knit Sleeves

With US 3 and Bamboo, cast on 57 (60, 63, 66, 69, 72). Knit 3 rows.

Knit 1 more row increasing 10 (11, 10, 11, 10, 11) sts evenly across as follows: k6 (5, 5, 8, 8, 6), m1 using a backwards loop cast on. *k5, (5, 6, 5, 6, 6), m1 with backwards loop. Repeat from * 9 (10, 9, 10, 9,10) times. End k6 (5, 4, 8, 7, 6). Total 67 (71, 73, 77, 79, 83) sts.

Change to US 5 needles and begin pattern stitch.

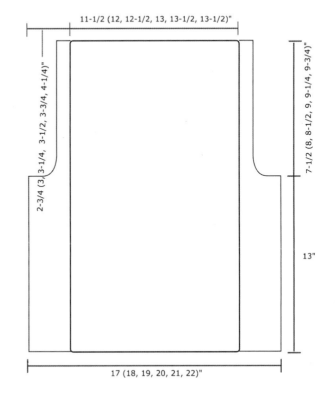

11-1/2 (12, 12-1/2, 13, 13-1/2, 13-1/2)"

2-3/4 (3, 3-1/4, 3-1/2, 3-3/4, 4-1/4)"

7-1/2 (8, 8-1/2, 9, 9-1/4, 9-3/4)"

13"

17 (18, 19, 20, 21, 22)"

PATTERN STITCH: (Edge stitch is sl1 knitwise on RS, sl1 purlwise on WS)

Row 1:1 Edge st, knit across.

Row 2:1 Edge st, purl across.

Row 3:1 Edge st, knit across.

Row 4:1 Edge st,*p2 tog. Repeat from * across.

Row 5:1 Edge st.,*yo (bring yarn over right hand needle and between needles to knit next st), k1. Repeat from * across.

Row 6:1 Edge st, purl across, purling into front of all yo's in order to twist the stitch. (I insert right hand needle into back of st, and slide it up and over left hand needle to front of st – easier).

Row 7: (inc row)1 Edge st, inc 1 in next st, knit to last 2 sts, inc 1 in next st, k1.

Row 8: 1 Edge st, knit across.

Repeat 8 row pattern stitch with inc on row 7, 4 more times.

*Complete 8 row pattern stitch with NO inc on row 7.

Repeat pattern stitch with inc on row 7.

Repeat from * above, once more, and finish with a NO increase repeat. Grand total of 10 pattern repeats and 81 (85, 87, 91, 93, 97) sts.

SLEEVE CAP: Continuing in pattern, bind off 5 (5, 5, 6, 6, 7) sts at the beginning of next 2 rows.

Bind off 2 sts at beginning of next 2 rows, slipping first st for a smoother curve. 67 (71, 73, 75, 77, 79) sts.

Edge st, ssk, work to last 3 sts, k2tog, k1 on all RS rows, 17 (18, 19, 20, 20, 21) times. To dec on row 5 of each pattern repeat (with yo's): edge st, *k1 yo. Repeat from * to last 2 sts, k2.

Work 0 (0, 0, 0, 2, 2) more rows. Slipping 1st st, bind off 2 sts at the beginning of the next 2 rows, and 3 sts at beginning of the next 4 rows. Bind off remaining 17 (19, 19, 19, 21, 21) sts.

Hand wash sleeves, pin to shape and dry flat. Although I like to steam iron my cotton blends, the Bamboo will not like the heat, so this will wet block the sleeves.

Finishing

Finish the top and bottom edges of woven pieces using folded hem with wide encased edge, p.25, #5.

With Zig Zag yarn, hand stitch front and back together at shoulder edges leaving a neck opening of 10-1/2 (11, 11-1/2, 12, 12-1/2, 12-1/2)".

Hand stitch side seams and sleeve underarm seams. Right sides showing, set in and hand stitch sleeve cap to armhole openings.

Sc across the bottom of knitted side panels to finish (optional). Weave in

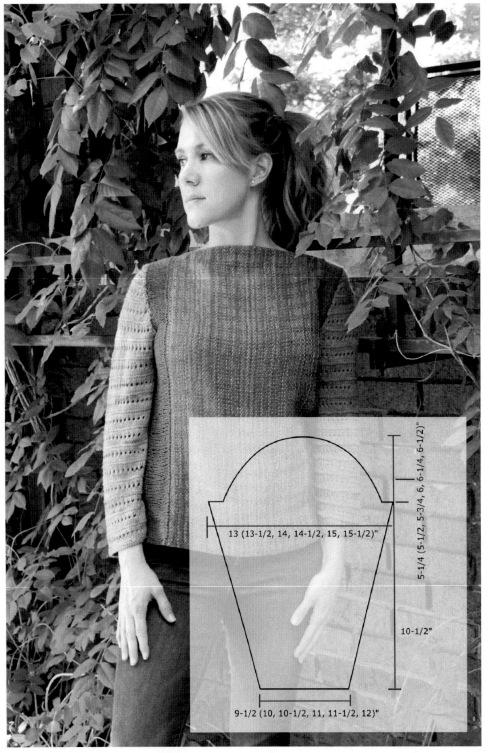

13 (13-1/2, 14, 14-1/2, 15, 15-1/2)"

5-1/4 (5-1/2, 5-3/4, 6, 6-1/4, 6-1/2)"

10-1/2"

9-1/2 (10, 10-1/2, 11, 11-1/2, 12)"

WRAPS

Sunset Poncho

Equipment

- 12 dent reed
- Warp sticks for wider warp (if desired, p.9)
- 2 shuttles
- Sewing machine
- Straight pins

Materials

- Schoppel Zauberball for lower piece weft, 1 ball #1536
- Cascade Heritage Sock for upper pieces & lower piece warp, 2 (2, 3) Skeins #5601
- Malabrigo Sock for lower piece warp, 1 skein Terracota
- Sewing thread

Skills Added

Zauberball's glorious transitional colorways practically weave this piece for you! Color blocks in this wearable poncho were created with thought given to the perfect proportions of the Euclidean golden ratio expressed as 1:1.6. Don't worry, you don't need to do the math to create this easy piece.

Weaving gauge		12 epi, 13-14 ppi		
To Fit Bust Sizes		**32-36"**	**38-42"**	**44-48"**
Yards	A Zauberball	368	408	445
	B Heritage Sock (Black)	694	811	922
	C Malabrigo Sock (Terracotta)	251	267	283
LOWER PIECE, MAKE 1				
Warp Length		94"	98"	102"
Warp Width		13-1/2"	14"	14-1/2"
# Warp Ends		162	168	174
UPPER PIECES, MAKE 2				
Warp Length		94"	98"	102"
Warp Width		8"	9"	10"
# Warp Ends		96	108	120
Weaving Length (lower piece)		70"	75"	79"
(each upper piece, make 2)		35"	37-1/2"	39-1/2"

To Warp Lower Piece, Warp Order (see Chart Reading, page 16)

B		66 (70, 74)
C	96 (98, 100)	

Weaving Instructions, Lower Piece

Weave lower piece alternating A and B according to weaving order at right. When complete, tie 6" fringe tassels at each end, p.21. In my piece, I edited some of tthe Zauberball colors, starting the weaving just after the first run of black by winding that off, and setting it aside. If you do that, and you need that length of yarn to finish, try to start it with a color that is close to the color where you end.

To Warp and Weave, Upper Pieces

Warp for 2 top pieces with Heritage Sock (B) and weave each piece to the length specified using the same for weft. Separate pieces by weaving 2 picks of scrap yarn in between. Raw finish <u>1 end</u> of each piece, p. 24, and <u>finish the other end of each piece with 6" fringe tassels</u>.

Weaving Order, Lower Piece (p.17)

A	B
3-1/2"	
	2-1/4"
1-1/4"	
	3-1/2"
49 (53, 57)"	
	3-1/2"
1-1/4"	
	2-1/4"
3-1/2"	

Sewing it together (measurements after washing)

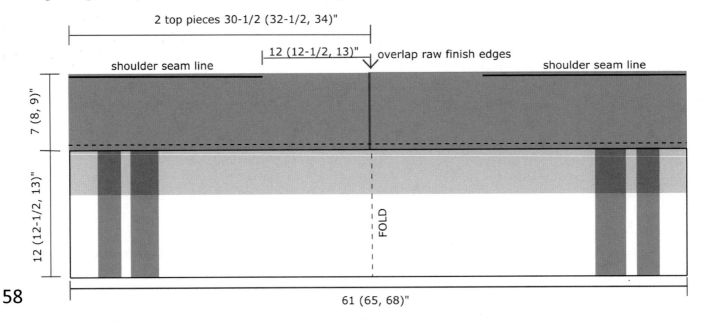

2 top pieces 30-1/2 (32-1/2, 34)"

12 (12-1/2, 13)" ↓ overlap raw finish edges

shoulder seam line   shoulder seam line

7 (8, 9)"

12 (12-1/2, 13)"

FOLD

61 (65, 68)"

Finishing

Wash and hang dry, all pieces, p. 26.

On long edges, overlap 2 top pieces over the lower piece 1/2", outside fringe edges matching as shown in diagram p.58. Overlap excess (if any) where the raw finish edges of top pieces meet at center.

Pin in place, and then baste in place. Sew 1 straight line across the top pieces from end-to-end, close to edges. See overlap seam, p.27.

SHOULDER SEAM: Fold right sides together at center line. Pin along top edge of the top pieces, leaving a neck opening of 12 (12-1/2, 13)" from center fold. Try on to see if neck opening suits you, then stitch shoulder seam with a minimal seam allowance along the 2nd thread from selvedge, sewing from neck opening to fringe edge.

Wear this with top pieces folded open around neckline to form a collar. Top pieces can be draped off one shoulder or down the front. Play with it, and have fun wearing!

Asymmetrical Cape

Equipment

- 12 dent reed
- 18-20 warp sticks (optional for wider warp, p.9)
- US 3, 24" or 32" circular knitting needles
- E or F crochet hook to pick up stitches
- Tapestry needle
- Sewing machine
- Straight pins

Materials

- Plymouth Yarn Co. Linaza, 2 skeins #8 Charcoal Grey/ Deep garnet, and 2 skeins #500 Black

Skills Added

Break out of the mold with this asymmetrical cape designed to drape off one shoulder with an armhole on the other side. I was delighted to find that these hand dyed skeins are dyed symmetrically making Plymouth's Linaza excellent for the palindrome warp, p.30. This allows the subtle color changes to pool together and refine the movement of the wrap.

You'll make one long piece and stitch together strategically, adding knitted lace at the neck opening. With this yarn, at this sett, I find approximately 7% shrinkage in width and 10 % in length.

Weaving Gauge: 12 epi, 13 ppi

Knitting Gauge: 19 sts/ 44 rows over 4" in pattern stitch

Size:		Sm	Med/Lg	xLg
To Fit Bust Sizes		32-36"	38-42"	44-48"
Yards	charcoal grey/deep garnet	686	846	873
	black	502	523	563
Warp Length		120"	150"	150"
Warp Width		14-1/2"	14-1/2"	15"
# Warp Ends		174	174	178
Weaving Length		96"	100"	104"

To Warp

With Charcoal Grey/Deep Garnet color, warp according to your size using the palindrome warp method, p.30. Warp lengths are approximate and may need to be adjusted to achieve striping effect. There will be some waste in the Med/Lg and xLg sizes.

Weaving Instructions

Plain weave using Black for weft, hemstitching the beginning and ending edges, p.22 - 23. Cut 8" fringe at each end, wash and hang dry, p.26.

Sewing it Together:

I realize the diagram, p.63, looks a little strange, but hang with me here as I take you through the steps to put your long rectangle together. There are just 2 places to seam.

A. Match up the 2 fringed edges and overlap for seaming as follows: measure 10 (11, 11)" from bottom. Overlap these selvedge edges by 1/2", Pin the overlap here and then pin (overlapping) 1-1/2" further. You should have approximately 63 (65, 69)" left around the neck opening. Hand baste the 1-1/2" between pins, and machine stitch this section close to edge. Backstitch to secure openings.

B. Measure 30 (31, 32)" along right side of neck opening. Mark the spot with a pin.

C. Measure 1-1/2" further and mark with a pin. Measure 20 (20, 22)" to make an armhole height of 10 (10, 11)". Mark this spot with a pin, and mark once more 1-1/2" further. Overlap the two 1-1/2" pin marked areas by 1/2", and pin them together. Before you hand baste and machine stitch this 1-1/2" overlap, check that there is approximately 10 (11, 12)" left (see D) along the neck opening from the last pin, to your starting point. Adjust armhole as necessary, then complete as per first overlapped seam.

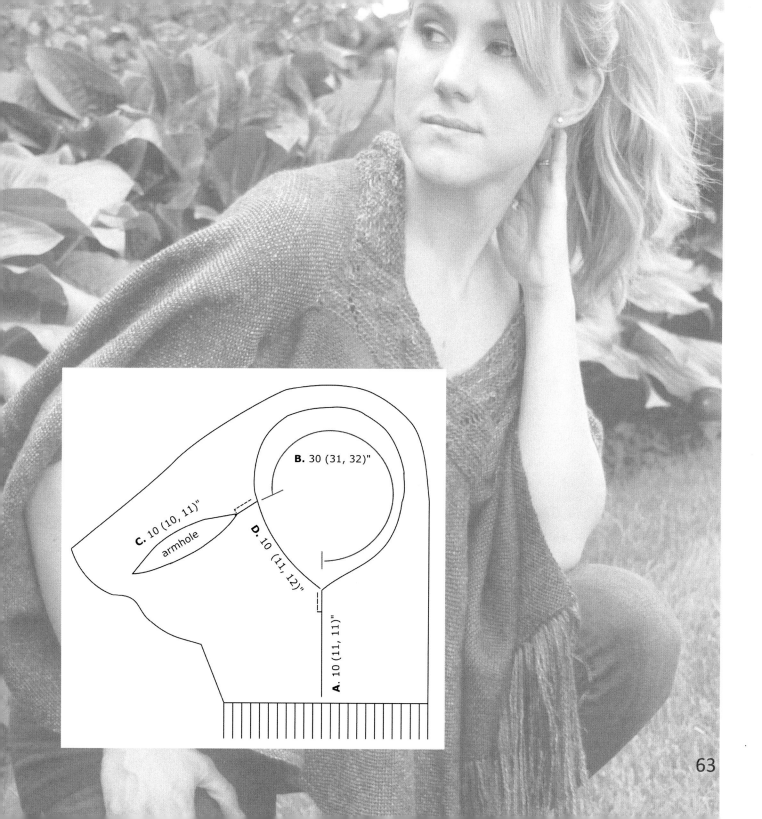

B. 30 (31, 32)"

C. 10 (10, 11)"
armhole

D. 10 (11, 12)"

A. 10 (11, 11)"

Knitting Instructions

Using the chart (read from right), lettered sts are at start and end of row only. For loose bind off, use "Grandma's Favorite Bind Off", p.29.

SHORT EDGE (D):

Pick up 50 (53, 59) sts, p.28, along short edge of neck opening (D). Knit 1 row (WS).

For size Sm: start with (b) and end with st #7 Repeat the 7 st pattern, 7 times across. Knit all even (WS) rows. Complete 22 rows, and bind off loosely.

For size Med/Lg: start with (a,b), repeat 7 st pattern 7 times, and end with (c,d). Knit all even (WS) rows. Complete 24 rows, and bind off loosely.

For size xLg: start with (b), repeat 7 st pattern 8 times, and end with (d). Knit all even (WS) rows. Complete 24 rows, and bind off loosely.

d	c	7	6	5	4	3	2	1	b	a	
	O	/					O	/			23
							O	/			21
						O	/				19
					O	/					17
				O	/						15
			O	/							13
		\	O								11
			\	O							9
				\	O						7
					\	O					5
						\	O				3
\	O						\	O			1

repeat 7 (7, 8)x - short edge

repeat 17(18,19)x -long edge

Chart shows RS only. Knit all WS rows.

\ = SSK
/ = K2tog
O = YO

LONG EDGE (B):

Pick up 123 (129, 134) sts along remaining (long edge, B) of neck opening. Knit 1 row, (WS).

For size Sm: start with (a,b), repeat 7 st pattern 17 times, ending with (c,d). Knit all even (WS) rows. Complete 22 rows, and bind off loosely.

For size Med/Lg: start with (b), repeat 7 st pattern 18 times, and end with (c,d). Knit all even (WS) rows. Complete 24 rows, and bind off loosely.

For size xLg: start with (b), repeat 7 st pattern from chart 19 times, and end with st #7. Knit all even (WS) rows. There will be a single st rather than a k2tog at last repeat on row 23. Complete 24 rows, and bind off loosely.

To wear, with fringe in front, place neck opening over head, slide right arm through armhole, and let neck opening drape off left shoulder to wrap around left arm.

Watercolor Kimono

Equipment

- 12 Dent Reed
- 18-20 warp sticks (optional for wider warp, p.9)
- Sewing Machine
- Sewing Needle

Materials

- Blue Heron Cotton Rayon Twist Lace for scarf and body warp, 1 skein Mossy Place
- Filatura Di Crosa Brilla for scarf and body warp, 2 balls #462 Teal
- Malabrigo Lace for scarf and body weft, 2 skeins Emerald
- Colinton Australia Lace Blends for sleeves, 2 skeins Cyprus
- 2-1/4 yds, 1/2" double fold bias seam tape
- Sewing Thread

Skills Added

This flattering and colorful, cropped kimono uses of one of my favorite warping techniques - the palindrome warp, p.30. Solid stripes of Filatura di Crosa Brilla between bands of Blue Heron's hand dyed lace weight add interest.

Add Colinton's luscious hand dyed kid mohair and silk to the sleeves to get a truly elegant effect. I found about 15% draw in and shrinkage, and 10% shrinkage in length with the scarf and body yarns, but lost very little width and length (about 3-4%) with the mohair. This is common with mohair as you don't need to pull your selvedges in as tight and it doesn't move much.

If you substitute something besides mohair for sleeves, *you will probably want to adjust the numbers on the sleeves to allow for around 15% take-up and shrinkage. To do this, divide the finished length and width (diagram p.68) by .85 for your new warp and weaving, length and width. Divide yards given for Colinton by .85 as well.*

ONE SIZE FITS MOST (size can be adjusted for width by pleat in back). For fuller bust, to add length, you may want to add 4" to the warp and weaving <u>lengths</u> of Body and Sleeve pieces. You should have enough extra yarn (22 yards to Sleeves and 11 yards each to Body yarns) in the skeins specified.

		Scarf	Body	Sleeves
Weaving Gauge		12 epi, 12 ppi	12 epi, 12 ppi	12 epi, 14 ppi
Yards	Cotton Rayon Twist Lace (CRTL)	693		
	Brilla	193		
	Malabrigo Lace	668		
	Colinton Lace Blends	468		
Warp Length		99"	99"	94"
Warp Width in Loom		12-1/2"	14-3/8"	8"
# Warp Ends		150	172	96
Weaving Length, Scarf		75"		
Weaving Length, Body, Sleeves (ea. piece, make 2)			37"	35"

To Warp, Scarf

		repeat 6x	
Brilla	6		6
CRTL		18	

With Brilla and Cotton Rayon Twist Lace (CRTL), warp for the scarf as given, following the warp order chart above. Use the Palindrome Warp method, p.30, but cutting and restarting with each Brilla stripe.

You will need to find the same pivot point each time you start a new CRTL stripe. Look at the apron rod when you do this, so you can match the color there when you restart. Remember that you don't need to make your color pools into perfect stripes. It will be more interesting if they aren't.

Weaving Instructions, Scarf

Plain weave with Malabrigo Lace to 75" Tie 6-8" tassels on each end as you remove from loom, p.21.

To Warp, Body

		repeat 6x	
Brilla	4		4
CRTL		24	

Weaving Instructions, Body (make 2)

Warp again in same palindrome/stripe fashion for the 2 Body pieces according to the variation above. Plain weave with Malabrigo Lace to 37", weave 2 picks of scrap yarn, and weave another piece to 37". Weave a 1/2" ending header with scrap yarn, and remove from the loom.

To Warp and Weave Sleeves (make 2)

Warp as given in beginning chart with Colinton Lace Blends only. Weave in plain weave with same yarn to 35" for each of the 2 pieces. Weave a 1/2" ending header and remove.

Raw finish all pieces of Sleeves and Body at both ends, p.24. Wash and hang dry or dry flat, p. 26.

When weaving with a sticky yarn like mohair (sleeves), you may want to insert a pick-up stick or warp stick into the back shed opening behind the reed to keep the warp "hairs" from felting together and preventing your shed from opening, p.20.

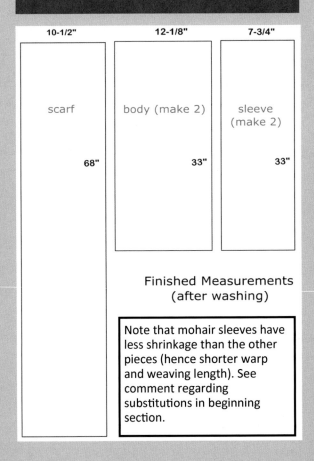

10-1/2"	12-1/8"	7-3/4"
scarf	body (make 2)	sleeve (make 2)
68"	33"	33"

Finished Measurements
(after washing)

Note that mohair sleeves have less shrinkage than the other pieces (hence shorter warp and weaving length). See comment regarding substitutions in beginning section.

Sewing it Together

Step 1. Overlap the 2 body pieces about 3/8" over the sleeve pieces to create overlap seams, p.27. Sew close to edge.

Step 2. Place 1 body piece over the other at center back, and create an overlap seam of about 3/8" for a length of 11" up from bottom edge. Pin, baste and machine stitch close to edge. Leave fronts open.

Step 3. Attach seam binding to begin folded hem with encased edge (p. 25, #4) continuous across the bottom of all joined bottom edges of back and do the same across the bottom edges of the 2 fronts. Fold in the 5/8" allowance at each end of seam binding and press., but do not hem yet.

Step 4. Place right sides together along the encased edges and sew <u>sleeves</u> together at underarm with a 5/8" allowance (see diagram). Press these seams open. Turn and press a 5/8" hem along the remaining, open encased edges. On inside, machine stitch along seam allowances and hems, close to edges of seam binding as shown at right. It is more important to keep your stitching consistent with the fabric edge than with the seam binding edge.

Step 5. Locate the center point of scarf piece along 1 long edge. Match this point to the center back at V opening. Pin scarf to RS of back and to front body pieces to hang even in front. Hand baste and machine stitch, pivoting at back V with a 1/4" seam allowance around. Reinforce the fabric at back V opening by sewing 1" either side of the V, just below the seam.

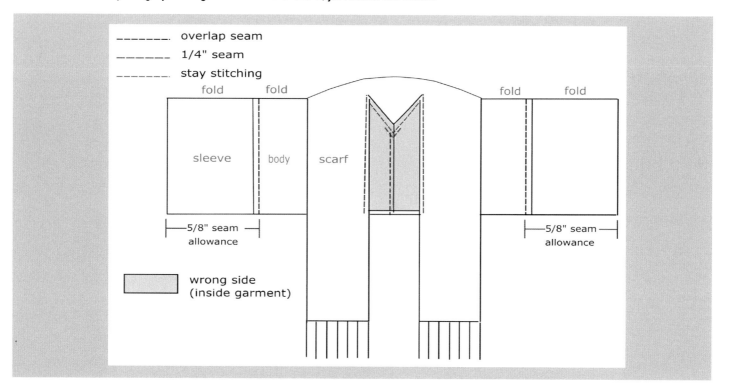

Sewing the Back Pleat:

On outside at center back seam, measure 1-1/4" to the right and fold right sides together from this point toward center. Make an accordian type fold back to right, and pin through all thicknesses. Repeat this in reverse to the left of center back seam. Baste in place, and machine stitch through all thicknesses. A walking foot will help with the bulk. If you need more ease around your mid section, you can make the pleat folds narrower.

Wear your kimono open in the front, or tie the scarf together as shown on the front cover.

VESTS

The Ashley Vest

Equipment

- 8 dent reed

- 18-20 warp sticks (optional for wider warp, p.9)

- US 5, 32" circular knitting needles

- US E or F crochet hook to pick up stitches

- tapestry needle to finish ends

- 3 locking stitch markers

- A row counter can be useful for the knitted portion.

Materials

- Blue Heron Cotton Rayon Seed, 2 (3, 3, 3) skeins - Cactus

Skills Added

Knitting lends graceful curves to this flattering vest, and the Blue Heron Cotton Rayon Seed grants it a wonderful texture! After weaving the lower rectangle, you'll pick up all your stitches for the top along one edge. The nubby texture of this yarn weaves best with a sett no closer than 8 epi.

Weaving gauge	8 epi, 9-10 ppi			
Knitting gauge	18 sts and 40 rows per inch in garter stitch (knit all rows)			
Size	Sm	Med	Lg	xLg
To Fit Bust Sizes	30-33"	34-37"	38-41"	42-45"
Yards	866	960	1070	1200
Warp Length	78"	81"	85"	88"
Warp Width	15"	15"	15"	15" (see p,17, for 15" warp)
# Warp Ends	120	120	120	120
Weaving Length	54"	58"	63"	68"

To Warp
Warp according to your size above.

Weaving Instructions
Weave a simple, plain weave rectangle.

Remove from loom, tying 6-8" long fringe tassels each side depending on your love of fringe. Wash and hang this piece dry before proceeding.

Knitted upper vest, back

Along 1 long edge of woven rectangle (this will be the RS top edge), mark center point of this edge, then measure 7 (8, 9, 10)" to the right of this center mark to begin picking up stitches. Pick up 63 (72, 81, 89) sts knitwise, working 14 (16, 18, 20)" from starting point to the left.

Knit 2 rows
Dec. row: ssk, knit to last 2 sts, K2tog.

Continue in garter stitch, repeating dec row every 3 rows 11 (13, 14, 14) MORE times, then every 6 rows 4 times total, 31 (36, 41, 49) sts. Knit 20 rows. Back piece will stretch when worn, so height is very approximate.

Back neck edge

(RS) Knit 9 (9, 9 12) sts, bind off 13 (18, 23, 25), Knit 9 (9, 9, 12) sts. Finishing left side separately, knit 1 row. Continuing in garter st, slip 1st st to bind off 3 (3, 3, 4) sts at neck edge 3 (3, 3, 3) times.

Attach yarn at right edge of back neck and finish as for left side reversing shaping.

Fronts and Collar

(Knit in one piece).
Attach yarn to far right on (RS) top edge of woven rectangle and pick up 68 (72, 76, 76) sts knit wise over 15 (16, 17, 17)".

Then with knitted cast on, add 48 (50, 51, 53) sts to the needles. Continue to pick up 34 (38, 44. 48) sts along back neck. Cast on another 48 (50, 51. 53) sts. Finish across by picking up 68 (72, 76, 76) sts starting 15 (16, 17, 17)" from left top edge of rectangle to end, 266 (282, 298, 306) sts.

Work in 2/2 Rib (Knit 2, Purl 2), ending Knit 2 for 4 (6, 8, 8) rows.

Begin Short Rows

I prefer the German short row technique, p.29. Use markers or safety pins to mark the double sts, if you have enough. You will need 30 (32, 34, 34) or, like me, you will get used to spotting the double st each time your approach it.

(RS) Work entire next row across in 2/2 rib pattern up to the 4th (6th, 8th, 8th) st from end of row, turn your work and perform double st as instructed, pm. Continue to work back across the row in pattern up to the 4th (6th, 8th, 8th) st from other end of row. Turn your work and repeat the double stitch effect at this end, pm.

Repeat these 2 rows, stopping to turn when you have worked through the 4th st before the last double st at each side (yes, there will be 3 sts between each double stitch) for a total of 15 (16, 17, 17) repeats.

On last turn (RS facing), work all the way to end of row working each of the double stitches created as one stitch as they appear removing markers as you complete. Complete one more row back across working each of the remaining double stitches on the other side as one.

Front Garter Panels

(WS) For first row, work first 60 (66, 72, 72) sts in garter, (place marker) continue across row in 2/2 rib as established, until you are 60 (66, 72, 72) sts before end of row, (place marker). Finish the row in garter.

Continue in this pattern for 32, (36, 26, 26) rows then see instructions for each size on page 76. Note – since row gauges can vary substantially among knitters, the depth of your knitted piece from the armhole opening should be approximately 6 ½ (7 ¼, 6, 6)" at this point. Add or subtract rows here to obtain this depth.

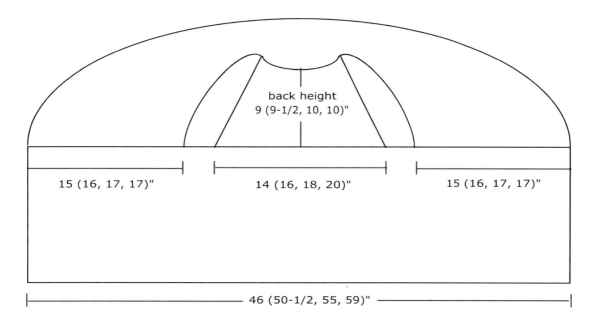

back height
9 (9-1/2, 10, 10)"

15 (16, 17, 17)"   14 (16, 18, 20)"   15 (16, 17, 17)"

46 (50-1/2, 55, 59)"

For all sizes when complete, use "Grandma's Favorite Bind Off", p.29.

For **Sm**, complete buttonhole rows next.

BUTTONHOLE: (RS), Work 64 (70, 76, 76) sts in established pattern, bind off 3 sts, resume pattern across. Next row: work to buttonhole edge, cast on 3 sts using knitted cast on through back loop (for tighter twist) and work to end of row in pattern.

Work 8 more rows in established pattern and bind off loosely.

For **Med**, complete buttonhole rows, then create dart near neck edge to control collar height as follows:

DART: on (RS), work 120 sts, turn and work double stitch for German short row, pm. Work back to beginning of row. *Work <u>through</u> 6th st before the double st marker, work double stitch for German short row, pm, and work back to beginning of row. Repeat from * 1 more time (total 3 repeats).

Next row: Work all the way across to the other front edge, removing short row markers as you work the double sts as one st. Repeat directions for dart on this side. Once this side is complete, resume pattern all the way across working double sts as one. Then bind off loosely .

For **Lg and xLg**,

DART: on (RS), work 126 sts, turn and work double stitch for German short row, pm. Work back to beginning of row. *Work through 6th st before the double st marker, work double stitch for German short row, pm, and work back to beginning of row. Repeat from * 5 more times (total 7 repeats). **AT THE SAME TIME**, on the 3rd repeat, complete buttonhole as given above. After all 7 short row repeats, next row: work all the way across to the other front edge, removing short row markers as you work the double sts as one st. Repeat directions for dart on this side. Once this side is complete, resume pattern all the way across working double sts as one. Then bind off loosely

Finishing:

Weave in ends. SC around armhole openings. Sew button on left front to correspond to buttonhole.

Tweed Vest

Equipment

- 10 dent reed

- 18-20 warp sticks (optional for wider warp, p.9)

- 2 shuttles

- Pick-up stick

- 18-20 warp sticks (optional for wider warp, p.9)

- US 3, 32" circular knitting needles

- US D or E crochet hook

- 2 locking stitch markers

- Tapestry needle to finish ends

Materials

Plymouth Yarn Co. Linazza, 2 (2, 2, 3) skeins #1350 Pine, and 1 (1,1, 2) skeins #500 Black

Skills Added

An unusual blend of Alpaca, Linen and Tencel, Linazza has a wonderful texture and touch, and yet enough body to give form to this geometric piece. Practice the 2 shuttle handling discussed on p. 15 to create a tweed effect. Note the subtle warp float accent along top edge created with the use of a pick-up stick.

I found about 7% width draw-in and shrinkage and 10% shrinkage in length with this fabric. You will weave 3 identical pieces, and add knitting where indicated. Fronts will hang open to drape diagonally.

		Sm	Med	Lg	xLg
Weaving gauge		10 epi, 16 ppi (this beat will create a firmer fabric)			
Knitting Gauge		19 sts/ 44 st over 4"			
Sizes		Sm	Med	Lg	xLg
To Fit Bust Sizes		32-34"	36-38"	40-42"	44-46"
Finished length	(after hemming, back at neck edge)	19-1/2"	20-1/2"	21"	21-1/2"
Back Shoulder Width	(finished w/ finished armhole)	12"	13-1/4"	14"	14-1/2"
Yards Pine		608	717	755	843
Black		349	382	445	461
Warp Length		**92"**	**95"**	**96"**	**98"**
Warp Width		**12-1/2"**	**13-3/4"**	**14-1/2"**	**15"**
#Warp Ends (periodic double warp adds to end count)		**168**	**184**	**192**	**200**
Weaving Length (each piece, make 3)		**22-1/4"**	**23-1/4"**	**24"**	**24-1/2"**

Troubleshooting the Weaving!   It is easy to accidentally place 2 colors in the same shed as you alternate colors in this piece. This will show up as a minor fabric flaw, so try to be conscious as you weave that Pine will go into the up shed, and Black will go into the down shed throughout.

To Warp, Warp Order

	repeat 4 (4, 5,5)x			repeat 13 (15, 14, 15)x			repeat 4 (4, 5, 5)x		
Hole		2				2				2
Slot	2	2		2	2	2		2	2	2	2

■ Charcoal   ■ Pine

Above, is a variation of the warp order chart when you need to consider both color changes as well as changing the way you draw your loops through holes <u>and</u> slots. You will draw 1 loop through the first slot, one through the hole to the left, then a loop through the next 2 slots in the color order indicated. You will be placing 8 ends in the span of 3 slots. I have not bothered to show the empty hole that comes after the second 2 loops in each color sequence on this chart (they are assumed).

When you sley the reed, this will make more sense. For each repeat, you will leave the first slot and hole as is, with two ends in each. Place 1 end from each of those next 2 loops into the hole to its left. This way each hole and slot will be filled, but there will be double warp at the beginning of each repeat – makes an interesting texture!

Weaving Instructions

Load a shuttle with each color. Weave each of 3 pieces, starting in the up shed and alternating 1 pick of Pine with 1 pick of Black. You can start the Black on the other side. Weave alternating for 20 (21, 21-1/2, 22)". End with Pine. See p.19 for tips on handling 2 shuttles.

Pick-up Pattern: Set the pick-up stick behind the reed as described on p.18, treating doubled warp threads as 1 end when you set the stick.

80

Assuming that you will throw the shuttle through the shed on each step, and that we will use the term heddle to mean the reed, weave the 8 step sequence below 2 times. Starting with Black, continue to alternate shuttles as follows: (Black will always be in the down shed.)

1. **Heddle down**
2. **Heddle up & Pick up Stick** (place the heddle in the up position and pull the pick-up stick forward (leaving it flat) to touch the reed
3. **Heddle down**
4. **Heddle up**
5. **Heddle down**
6. **Heddle up & Pick up Stick**
7. **Heddle down**
8. **Heddle up**

Once you've completed the 8 steps twice through, remove the pick up stick and continue plain weave, alternating colors as before until the piece is the length given for your size.

Between the 3 pieces, weave 2 picks of scrap yarn. Weave a 1/2" of scrap ending header when you are done. Remove from the loom and raw finish all edges, p.24. before cutting the pieces apart.

Wash all pieces and hang dry or dry flat.

<u>Complete encased edge</u> on top end of all pieces

Knitting Instructions:

<u>The pick-up pattern in the woven pieces are not the same on both sides of the fabric, so make sure you identify right and wrong sides for all pieces.</u>

On RS selvedge of first piece (this will be the back piece), measure 8 (8-1/2, 9, 9-1/2))" from top edge and pm. Pick up 57 (59, 61, 63) sts between marker and up to 1/2" away from bottom edge (allowed for hemming later).

**Finished measurements of back piece
after seaming and hemming
(before crochet finish)**

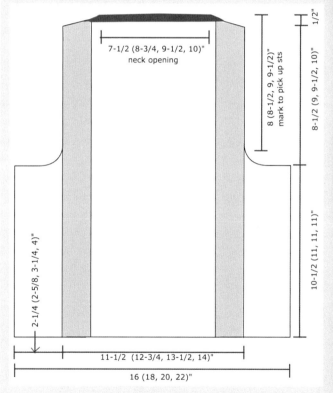

7-1/2 (8-3/4, 9-1/2, 10)"
neck opening

1/2"

8 (8-1/2, 9, 9-1/2)"
mark to pick up sts

8-1/2 (9, 9-1/2, 10)"

10-1/2 (11, 11, 11)"

2-1/4 (2-5/8, 3-1/4, 4)"

11-1/2 (12-3/4, 13-1/2, 14)"

16 (18, 20, 22)"

Work in garter stitch, decreasing 1 st at armhole edge 5 times, then work straight to total 25, (29, 36, 44) rows measuring 2-1/4 (2 -5/8, 3-1/4, 4)" from selvedge. Bind off, and repeat on other side of this piece.

Place remaining 2 front pieces RS up, marking 8 (8-1/2, 9, 9-1/2))" from top edge to pick up 57 (59, 61, 63) sts on right selvedge of one piece and the same on left selvedge of the other piece. Complete garter rows as above, and bind off.

81

Finishing

Go to p. 26-27 for instructions on how to create my sloped shoulder overlap.

Overlap at armhole edge will be 1".

Shoulder length measurement will be 2".

With back over RS of front, complete sloped shoulder seam on each side.

Sew side seams together and hem bottom edges of weaving using lace seam binding finish, p.25, #6.

With Pine, sc 2 rnds around armhole openings and 1 row across bottom edge of knitted side panels.

ACCESSORIES

3-2-1 COWL
& matching
TOTE

Equipment

- 8 dent reed

- 2 Shuttles

Materials

- Multi: Filatura Di Crosa Mini Tempo, 1 ball for Cowl and 1 ball for Tote in #43 Meadow,

- Solid: Interlacements Zig Zag, 1 skein for Cowl and 1 skein for Tote in Black

- Cellophane, masking, or repositionable tape for cowl finishing

Extra Equipment and Materials For Tote:

- Size F crochet hook
- Sewing Machine
- 4 pieces 12" x 9" high quality felt
- One 1-1/4" button
- Handles approx. 14" wide or Straps
- 1 Yard Pellon Craft Fuse Stabilizer
- Sewing Thread

Skills Added (Tote)

Named for the proportion of long vertical stripes, this cowl can be worn long as shown at left, double it, or leave it untied, and hang it as a scarf. The matching tote sports handcrafted wooden handles, or add a shoulder strap instead, shown p.87 and p.89.

		Cowl	Tote
Weaving gauge	10 epi, 10 ppi		
MiniTempo yds.		145	95
Zig Zag yds.		365	409
Warp Length		**87"**	**88"**
Warp Width in Loom		**12-1/2"**	**12-1/2"**
# Warp Ends		**124**	**124**
Weaving Length		**63"**	**36-1/2" Tote side piece**
			13-1/2" Base piece

To Warp Cowl, Warp Order (see Chart Reading, page 16)

Solid	4		10		20		30
Multi		30		20		10	

Cowl Weaving Instructions

Wind a shuttle with each color. Weave according to chart at right.

Tie 3 strand tassels, 8" long, p.21. To connect the cowl ends, with both ends knotted and trimmed, twist the rectangle one time for a mobius effect, and tape each end to your work table facing each other, 2" apart. Tie a double knot with a tassel from one end and the corresponding tassel of the other end in the middle. This allows a 1" gap of fringe either side of this knot for an open effect at the join.

Solid	Multi
4"	
	1/2"
54"	
	1/2"
4"	

Wear your cowl long or doubled

To Warp Tote

Warp with your solid color as given on p.85.

Tote Weaving Instructions

Weave in plain weave, changing colors with solid and multi in the order given in chart at right (read top to bottom). MEASURE CAREFULLY TO GET THE BEST FIT WHEN YOU PUT THIS TOGETHER.

When finished, you will weave a 1/2" scrap header, unwind this piece from front, pull the warp threads forward a bit, and cut this piece from the loom, close to the header. DO NOT REMOVE THE WARP FROM THE REED. YOU WILL REUSE IT.

Some weavers will weave the narrower piece without removing the wider one, but I don't like to have to mess with unused warp threads getting in my way as I weave.

Here's how you reset the warp:

Holding the ends together, unwind the warp all the way until you can get at the back apron rod. For the next piece, isolate the warp that goes through the center 5" in the reed, and remove the other ends from the rod to discard.

Step back and tie an overhand knot near the cut ends of the warp you have preserved, trying to keep them the same length so the warp threads remain reasonably centered around the back rod. Wind on, repacking your warp again. Tie to the front rod. .

After weaving your new header to space the warp threads again, weave this narrower warp with solid. Plain weave for 13 ½".

Weave an ending header and remove from loom. Raw finish edges of both pieces, EXCEPT you will round out your corners by sewing around the edges when you finish the base piece. This will make it fit better when you attach the body.

Multi	Solid
2-3/4"	
	2-1/4"
8-3/4"	
	2-1/4"
4-1/2"	
	2-1/4"
8-3/4"	
	2-1/4"
2-3/4"	

Trim close to stitching. Washing is optional for non-wearables.

Construction

Press the pieces to block. Cut Pellon to correspond to each of your 2 pieces, but 1/2" smaller on all sides, and pin in place. With the shiny side of Pellon facing up, place your fabric over it. Using a wet pressing cloth on top and the wool setting on your iron, fuse the interfacing to the fabric. Use a side to side motion in a small area for 10-15 seconds. Interfacing may not adhere in some places, but it will hold substantially in place until you can get the pieces sewn together.

TOTE BODY: With right sides together, match up the raw finished edges. Pin the solid stripes of each side together to insure that you get a good match front and back as you do this. Sew the bag body side seam, checking to see that the side stripe of the multi at this seam will end up the same size as the multi stripe at the other side of bag before you sew it together. I've allowed for a 1/2" side seam, but adjust as needed.

Press the side seam open. Turn the top edge (1/2") of bag body over the Pellon edge, press and machine stitch in place. If you want the knitted handle tabs on your purse (instructions p.88), leave a slack edge before you sew the fabric over the Pellon, so it is easier to pick up stitches.

ADDING THE BASE: Bag body is still inside out. Turn the body, upside down, and pin the RS of base piece to the right side of the body piece to fit around the inner edge. If you center each end of the base at the side (multi) stripes, it is then easier to center and pin the long sides. Hand baste in place close to edge. Machine stitch the pieces together using a 1/2" seam allowance and a long basting stitch. If satisfied with the fit, sew this seam a 2nd time around with a shorter stitch to secure.

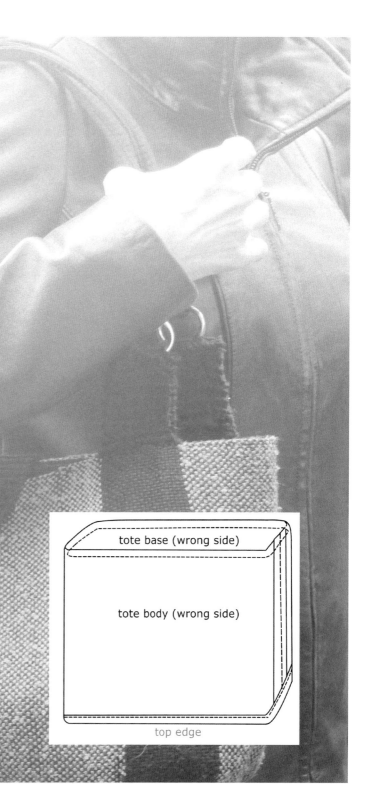

tote base (wrong side)

tote body (wrong side)

top edge

Turn bag right side out.

Knitted Handle Tabs (eliminate if adding shoulder straps directly to side of tote)

On outside of tote at top edge along the solid stripe, pick up 14 sts. Knit 37 rows in garter (19 garter ridges on right side) ending with wrong side row. Turn work and fold wrong sides together.

TO FUSE THE TAB SHUT: with the left hand needle, lift the first lower loop of the garter ridge that is just above the cast on edge to make a new st. Knit this new st together with the st on the needle to the left. Repeat this with the next garter loop and bind off by slipping the first st over the 2nd, Repeat across.

Cut a long tail to whip stitch the bound off edge to tote edge to reinforce. Repeat on all 4 solid stripes.

Knitted Closure

Cast on 4 sts.

Row 1: Knit 1 row.

Row 2: Knit 1, m1. Knit up to last st, m1, K1

Repeat rows 1 and 2 above until 14 sts on needle.

BUTTONHOLE: Knit 6 sts, bind off 2, knit 6. On left side of bind off, knit 5 rows, cast on 2 sts, and place on stitch holder, leaving yarn attached.. WS still facing, attach a separate length of yarn to the other side of bind off, and knit 4 rows. Turn work, place sts from holder back onto needles. Using working yarn from the first side, knit across the 2nd side.

Knit 30 more rows (16 garter ridges). Bind off leaving a long tail to stitch flap to center back of purse approximately 2" below purse edge. Attach button on opposite for closure. Weave in all knitting ends.

Easy to Make Liner

This tote is just the right size to take advantage of standard size pieces of felt to make a quick liner. I order high quality wool felt on Etsy (*www.etsy.com*) in 12" x 9" pieces. These require no hemming and make a nice firm liner.

Cut 2 of the pieces according to the following diagrams.

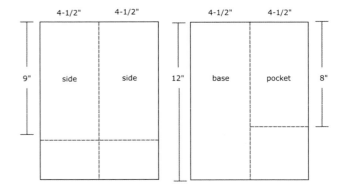

Center the pocket piece along one of the long sides of a full piece about 1/2" below top edge, and stitch around sides and bottom. Pocket will sit better if you pull the pocket piece taut, but ease about 1/8" slack in the body piece each side when you sew it in place.

Now take the full pieces, and sew them to the side pieces along the 9" edges (RS's together) to make a box. Allow 1/4" seam allowance.

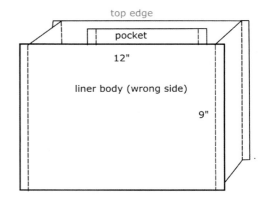

Round off the corners of your base piece with your scissors, turn your liner box upside down, and set the base into the bottom edge of your liner box. Pin, baste, and stitch the base in place (the same way you did your tote base).

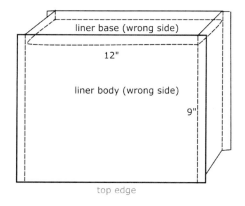

liner base (wrong side)

12"

liner body (wrong side)

9"

top edge

Drop the liner into the tote (wrong sides together). Whipstitch in place around the top edge, put a stitch in each bottom corner to tack the bag and liner together, and you are done!

Pillars and Hedgerows Scarf

Equipment

- 8 dent reed
- 2 Shuttles
- 15" Pick-up Stick

Materials

- Color A: Shalimar Yarns Breathless DK, 1 skein Saffron

- Color B: Interlacements Zig Zag, 1 skein Black

Challenge yourself a little with a variation on log cabin weave combined with a pick-up stick pattern to create weft floats. This one has a somewhat higher degree of difficulty. A scarf for him or her, it's reversible with a slightly different design on each side to make it more interesting. You get almost 20% draw-in and shrinkage in this piece. See p. 15 for advice on handling 2 shuttles.

Weaving Gauge: 8 epi, 11 ppi in log cabin sections. Closer in areas with weft floats.

Finished Measurements		8-1/2" x 58"
Yards	Breathless DK (A)	252
	Zig Zag (B)	247
	Warp Length	96"
	Warp Width	10-5/8"
	#Warp Ends	85
	Weaving Length	72"

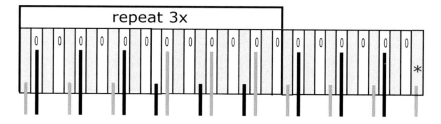

To Warp

Here's a different type of chart for you! To set up log cabin with a direct warp, begin pulling your loops according the drawing above, alternating colors as shown. The thick lines represent a loop of 2 strands, except for the one marked with * at right. This will be 1 strand pulled through a slot, then cut and tied off at the warping peg. Next, from right, you will skip 1 hole and 1 slot, pull 1 loop in a hole, 1 in a slot, then skip 1 hole and 1 slot...repeat across according to chart. Notice that after every 6th loop, the sequence of color changes, placing 2 of the same colors next to each other.

Wind yarn onto the loom. To sley the reed, see p.92.

Log Cabin is simply a result of alternating colors in warp and weft. Wherever 2 ends of the same color are next to each other, the pattern appears to change direction.

Sleying the reed:

This is the step that sets up the magic!

Facing front of loom and starting at right, sley 1 hole thread into the empty hole to left. Sley 1 slot thread into the empty slot to left. This will fill in all the skipped spaces (see below). Repeat this action across. You will end up with Black threads in the first 6 holes, Saffron threads in the first 6 slots. Then there will be Saffron ends in the next 6 holes, Black threads in the next 6 slots. Alternate this way across, and end with the 1 additional Saffron end which makes your selvedge ends the same color.

The only challenge at this stage is to be careful to keep the threads from excessive crossing in the back as you pull them through the slots. You won't need to cut them as you change color. The photo below shows you how this should look as you begin to sley the reed.

Setting the pick-up stick:

See page 18. Leave the stick in the warp throughout weaving.

Ready to Weave!

Wind a shuttle with each color. After your header is done, start at right, in the up shed, with B. Rather than tucking your starting tail into the next shed after the first pick, as we often do, I recommend that you wrap the tail around the outermost warp thread and tuck it into the same shed as the first pick. This hides the tail better when you are alternating colors.

Next start color B on the left, tucking that tail into the same shed that you throw from (as you did on the right side).

Following the chart at right, you have just completed the 1st repeat of sequence #1 which you will repeat a total of 6 times. The chart will tell you the color by column and which shed to open (up or down) for that color. Continue working the chart downward through #2, 6 times. Whenever the 2 shuttles are on the same side, it is important to wrap the threads in a way that keeps the next pick from missing the outermost warp thread. See p.19 for advice on handling 2 shuttles.

At sequence #3, here's how you do your "pick-up" row:

Put the reed in the neutral position in back. Pull the pick-up stick forward and place it <u>upright</u> against the reed. This opens a special shed. Throw Saffron through, move the stick back to its resting position on the back beam, so you can move the reed to the up position for the next throw, and continue to follow the weaving order downward.

NOTE – Manage edges on pick-up rows as needed. When you throw a pick through a special pick-up row, it sometimes misses the outer warp thread at one end or another of that pick. In this case, wrapping the threads together may still not be the solution. If so, just wrap the shuttle around the outermost warp thread before your throw - problem solved. Once you figure this out, you'll see this

Weaving Order:

		A	B
			UP
1	6X	DOWN	
		UP	
2	6X		DOWN
		PICK-UP	
	2X		UP
		DOWN	
	2X		UP
		PICK-UP	
3	2X		UP
		DOWN	
		REPEAT #2	
		REPEAT #1	
		REPEAT #3	
			DOWN

End with rep #1 on #11 ☞

happen in the same place throughout. You can work faster if you anticipate this. If you started your yarns as I did, you will find that this happens at the left side of the first 2 pick-up rows in sequence #3 (the first time through each repeat).

So I've given you a few things to think about, but proceed slowly at first, you'll get the hang of it and have fun! Also, go to www.poffstudio.com for a free downloadable chart like the one below to place by your side, follow the weaving order easily, and keep track your progress.

		A	B	repeats										
				1	2	3	4	5	6	7	8	9	10	11
			UP											
1	6X	DOWN												
		UP												
2	6X		DOWN											
		PICK-UP												
	2X		UP											
		DOWN												
	2X		UP											
		PICK-UP												
3	2X		UP											
		DOWN												
		REPEAT #2												
		REPEAT #1												
		REPEAT #3												
			DOWN											

End with rep #1 on #11 ☞

Books:

What makes the study of rigid heddle weaving so dynamic is that there are so many different the ways to get things done right! As teachers, we never stop learning from each other and from our students, so I encourage you to continue your learning, and share your discoveries. The following publications are some of my favorite references for expanding your study.

Weave, Knit, Wear

By Judith Shangold, XRX, Inc.

Lovely garment designs for rigid heddle looms using 4-1/2" -20" weaving widths. Judith also does a nice job of covering the basics of weaving, along with knitting, sewing, fit, and finishing techniques. Includes design and color choice ideas.

Inventive Weaving on a Little Loom

By Syne Mitchell, Storey Publishing

This book gives you a broad and detailed perspective on rigid heddle weaving, from the very elementary steps to the advanced level of multi heddle weaving. I like that Syne covers the physical, mental, and emotional aspects of our craft.

The Weavers Idea Book

By Jane Patrick, Interweave

This one is the definitive reference of almost every weave we can accomplish on the rigid heddle loom. Some patterns included. A must for every weaving library in hard cover. I love that it is spiral bound to sit flat on your work table.

Woven Scarves

By Jane Patrick and Stephanie Flynn Sokolov, Interweave

The beauty of this book is that they cover so many different fibers, fabric finishes, and treatments: from felting to discharge dying, adding things like beads and pom poms along the way. Basics are covered in the back. You'll also find a suggestion for how to determine the yardage of stash yarns.

Videos:

The Ultimate Rigid-Heddle Weaving Digital Bundle

Videos by Liz Gipson, Interweave.com

Liz is my go to girl for visuals that make all things rigid heddle look easy. If you like visual instruction, this package from Interweave will take you from beginner to advanced technique.

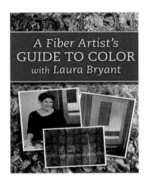

A Fiber Artist's Guide to Color

By Laura Bryant, Interweave.com

In this video, Laura Bryant, the creative founder of Prism Yarns, has given us a color system to make confident choices for weaving. Combining color theory and naturally occurring phenomena, she assigns a new language and structure to color selection for beautiful results.

BOOKS & VIDEOS

Yarns and Yarn Companies featured:

Check websites for a list of list of their retailers.

BE SWEET

www.besweetproducts.com

Mango Moon Yarns

      Bamboo, 100% hand dyed bamboo; 50 gm = 110 yds

BLUE HERON YARNS

www.blueheronyarns.com,

      Cotton Rayon Seed, 68% rayon, 32% cotton; 8 oz = 450 yds

      Cotton Rayon Twist Lace, 25% cotton, 75% rayon; 8 oz =1000 yds

      Organic Cotton, 100% organic cotton; 8 oz = 630 yds

      Silk Linen, 65% silk, 35% linen; 4 oz = 750 yds

CASCADE

www.cascadeyarns.com

      Heritage Sock, 75% superwash merino wool, 2% nylon; 100 gm = 437 yds

COLINTON AUSTRALIA

www.colintonaustralia.com

      Lace Blends, 80% unbrushed mohair, 20% silk, hand dyed; 50 gm = 250 yds

FILATURA DI CROSA

www.tahkistacycharles.com

Tahki Stacy Charles Inc.

      Brilla, 58% viscose, 42% cotton; 50 gm = 120 yds

      MiniTempo, 45% cotton, 36% acrylic, 19% nylon; 50 gm = 180 yds

HAMILTON YARNS

www.hamiltonyarns.com

Heaven's Hand, Shaman, 100% hand spun, hand dyed raw silk; 50 gm = 330 yds

INTERLACEMENTS YARNS

www.interlacementsyarns.com

Cabled Cotton, 100% mercerized cotton; 4 oz = 270 yds

Irish Linen, 40% linen, 31% cotton, 29% rayon; 8 oz = 600 yds

Zig Zag, 100% rayon; 8 oz = 500 yds

MALABRIGO

www.malabrigoyarn.com

Lace, 100% baby merino wool; 50 gm = 470 yds

Sock, 100% superwash wool; 100 gm = 440 yds

PLYMOUTH YARN COMPANY, INC.

www.plymouthyarn.com

Linaza, 50% alpaca, 25% linen, 25% tencel; 100 gm = 440 yds

SHALIMAR YARNS

www.shalimaryarns.com

Breathlesss DK, 75% sw merino, 15% cashmere, 10% silk; 100 gm = 270 yds

SCHOPPEL YARN

www.skacelknitting.com

Skacel Collection, Inc. (also source for Addi Clicks Crochet Hooks)

Zauberball, 75% superwash wool, 25% nylon; 100 gm = 460 yds

YARNS

While I have toiled and obsessed over the patterns in this book, alas - weavers will weave differently, and I am but an imperfect human being at any rate. If you find errors or problems herein, please contact me through my website, *www. Poffstudio.com*, where I can post errata if needed. Please also let me know about your weaving triumphs, and help yourself to free patterns there for your use.